The Logic of Business Decision Making

THE LOGIC OF BUSINESS DECISION MAKING

A Harvard Business Review Paperback

Harvard Business Review paperback No. 90046

ISBN 0-87584-287-9

The *Harvard Business Review* articles in this collection are available as individual reprints with the exception of "Quantitative Techniques for Today's Decision Makers." Discounts apply to quantity purchases. For information and ordering contact Operations Department, Harvard Business School Publishing Division, Boston, MA 02163. Telephone: (617) 495-6192, 9 a.m. to 5 p.m. Eastern Standard Time, Monday through Friday. Fax: (617) 495-6985, 24 hours a day.

Editor's Note: Some articles in this book may have been written before authors and editors began to take into consideration the role of women in management. We hope the archaic usage representing all managers as male does not detract from the usefulness of the collection.

Printed in the United States of America by Harvard University, Office of the University Publisher.
93 92 91 5 4 3 2 1

Contents

Quantitative Decision Making

Decision Trees
for
Decision Making

▶ *Helpful in identifying choices, risks, gains, goals.*
▶ *Applicable in many important areas of investment.*

By John F. Magee

The management of a company that I shall call Stygian Chemical Industries, Ltd., must decide whether to build a small plant or a large one to manufacture a new product with an expected market life of ten years. The decision hinges on what size the market for the product will be.

Possibly demand will be high during the initial two years but, if many initial users find the product unsatisfactory, will fall to a low level thereafter. Or high initial demand might indicate the possibility of a sustained high-volume market. If demand is high and the company does not expand within the first two years, competitive products will surely be introduced.

If the company builds a big plant, it must live with it whatever the size of market demand. If it builds a small plant, management has the option of expanding the plant in two years in the event that demand is high during the introductory period; while in the event that demand is low during the introductory period, the company will maintain operations in the small plant and make a tidy profit on the low volume.

Management is uncertain what to do. The company grew rapidly during the 1950's; it kept pace with the chemical industry generally. The new product, if the market turns out to be large, offers the present management a chance to push the company into a new period of profitable growth. The development department, particularly the development project engineer, is pushing to build the large-scale plant to exploit the first major product development the department has produced in some years.

The chairman, a principal stockholder, is wary of the possibility of large unneeded plant capacity. He favors a smaller plant commitment, but recognizes that later expansion to meet high-volume demand would require more investment and be less efficient to operate. The chairman also recognizes that unless the company moves promptly to fill the demand which develops, competitors will be tempted to move in with equivalent products.

The Stygian Chemical problem, oversimplified as it is, illustrates the uncertainties and issues that business management must resolve in making investment decisions. (I use the term "investment" in a broad sense, referring to outlays not only for new plants and equipment but also for large, risky orders, special marketing facilities, research programs, and other purposes.) These decisions are growing more important at the same time that they are increasing in complexity. Countless executives want to make them better — but how?

In this article I shall present one recently developed concept called the "decision tree," which has tremendous potential as a decision-making tool. The decision tree can clarify for management, as can no other analytical tool that I know of, the choices, risks, objectives, monetary gains, and information needs involved in an investment problem. We shall be hearing a great deal about decision trees in the years ahead. Although a novelty to most businessmen today, they will surely be in common management parlance before many more years have passed.

Later in this article we shall return to the problem facing Stygian Chemical and see how management can proceed to solve it by using decision trees. First, however, a simpler example will illustrate some characteristics of the decision-tree approach.

Displaying Alternatives

Let us suppose it is a rather overcast Saturday morning, and you have 75 people coming for cocktails in the afternoon. You have a pleasant garden and your house is not too large; so if the weather permits, you would like to set up the refreshments in the garden and have the party there. It would be more pleasant, and your guests would be more comfortable. On the other hand, if you set up the party for the garden and after all the guests are assembled it begins to rain, the refreshments will be ruined, your guests will get damp, and you will heartily wish you had decided to have the party in the house. (We could complicate this problem by considering the possibility of a partial commitment to one course or another and opportunities to ad-

EXHIBIT I. DECISION TREE FOR COCKTAIL PARTY

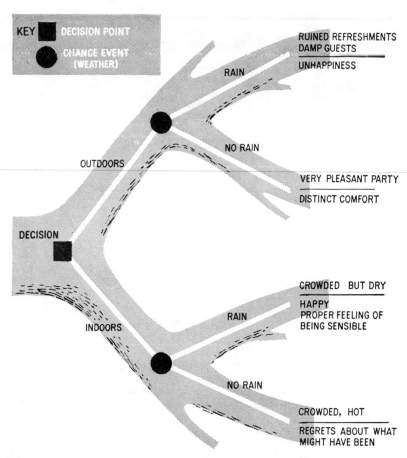

just estimates of the weather as the day goes on, but the simple problem is all we need.)

This particular decision can be represented in the form of a "payoff" table:

	Events and Results	
Choices	Rain	No Rain
Outdoors	Disaster	Real comfort
Indoors	Mild discomfort, but happy	Mild discomfort, but regrets

Much more complex decision questions can be portrayed in payoff table form. However, particularly for complex investment decisions, a different representation of the information pertinent to the problem — the decision tree — is useful to show the routes by which the various possible outcomes are achieved. Pierre Massé, Commissioner General of the National Agency for Productivity and Equipment Planning in France, notes:

"The decision problem is not posed in terms of an isolated decision (because today's decision depends on the one we shall make tomorrow) nor yet in terms of a sequence of decisions (because under uncertainty, decisions taken in the future will be influenced by what we have learned in the meanwhile). The problem is posed in terms of a tree of decisions." [1]

EXHIBIT I illustrates a decision tree for the cocktail party problem. This tree is a different way of displaying the same information shown in the payoff table. However, as later examples will show, in complex decisions the decision tree is frequently a much more lucid means of presenting the relevant information than is a payoff table.

The tree is made up of a series of nodes and branches. At the first node on the left, the host has the choice of having the party inside or outside. Each branch represents an alternative course of action or decision. At the end of each branch or alternative course is another node representing a chance event — whether or not it will rain. Each subsequent alternative course to the right represents an alternative outcome of this chance event. Associated with each complete alternative course through the tree is a payoff, shown at the end of the rightmost or terminal branch of the course.

When I am drawing decision trees, I like to indicate the action or decision forks with square nodes and the chance-event forks with round ones. Other symbols may be used instead, such as single-line and double-line branches, special letters, or colors. It does not matter so much which method of distinguishing you use so long as you do employ one or another. A decision tree of any size will always combine (a) *action* choices with (b) different possible *events* or *results* of action which are partially affected by chance or other uncontrollable circumstances.

Decision-Event Chains

The previous example, though involving only a single stage of decision, illustrates the elementary principles on which larger, more complex decision trees are built. Let us take a slightly more complicated situation:

You are trying to decide whether to approve a development budget for an improved product. You are urged to do so on the grounds that the development, if successful, will give you a competitive edge, but if you do not develop the product, your competitor may — and may seriously damage your market share. You sketch out a decision tree that looks something like the one in EXHIBIT II.

Your initial decision is shown at the left. Following a decision to proceed with the project, if development is successful, is a second stage of decision at Point A. Assuming no important change in the situation between now and the time of Point A, you decide now what alternatives will be important to you at that time. At the right of the tree are the outcomes of different sequences of decisions and events. These outcomes, too, are based on your present information. In effect you say, "If what I know now is true then, this is what will happen."

Of course, you do not try to identify all the events that can happen or all the decisions you will have to make on a subject under analysis. In the decision tree you lay out only those decisions and events or results that are important to you and have consequences you wish to compare. (For more illustrations, see the APPENDIX.)

Adding Financial Data

Now we can return to the problems faced by the Stygian Chemical management. A decision tree characterizing the investment problem as outlined in the introduction is shown in EXHIBIT III (page 7). At Decision #1 the company must decide between a large and a small plant. This is all that must be decided *now*. But if the company chooses to build a small plant and then finds demand high during the initial period, it can in two years — at Decision #2 — choose to expand its plant.

But let us go beyond a bare outline of alternatives. In making decisions, executives must take account of the probabilities, costs, and returns which appear likely. On the basis of the data now available to them, and assuming no important change in the company's situation, they reason as follows:

❪ Marketing estimates indicate a 60% chance of a large market in the long run and a 40% chance of a low demand, developing initially as follows:

Initially high demand, sustained high:	60%
Initially high demand, long-term low:	10% ⎫
Initially low and continuing low:	30% ⎬ Low = 40%
Initially low and subsequently high:	0% ⎭

❪ Therefore, the chance that demand initially will be high is 70% (60 + 10). *If* demand is

[1] *Optimal Investment Decisions: Rules for Action and Criteria for Choice* (Englewood Cliffs, New Jersey, Prentice-Hall, Inc., 1962), p. 250.

EXHIBIT II.   DECISION TREE WITH CHAINS OF ACTIONS AND EVENTS

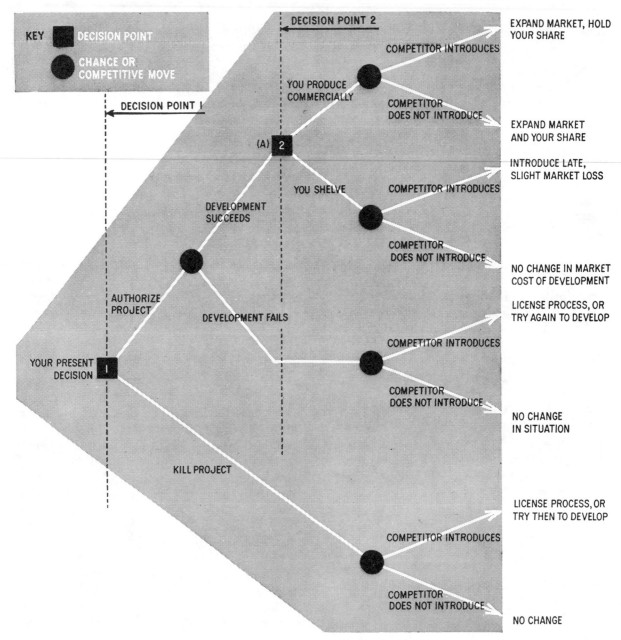

high initially, the company estimates that the chance it will continue at a high level is 86% (60 ÷ 70). Comparing 86% to 60%, it is apparent that a high initial level of sales changes the estimated chance of high sales in the subsequent periods. Similarly, if sales in the initial period are low, the chances are 100% (30 ÷ 30) that sales in the subsequent periods will be low. Thus the level of sales in the initial period is expected to be a rather accurate indicator of the level of sales in the subsequent periods.

❡ Estimates of annual income are made under the assumption of each alternative outcome:

1. A large plant with high volume would yield $1,000,000 annually in cash flow.

2. A large plant with low volume would yield only $100,000 because of high fixed costs and inefficiencies.

3. A small plant with low demand would be economical and would yield annual cash income of $400,000.

4. A small plant, during an initial period of high demand, would yield $450,000 per year, but this would drop to $300,000 yearly in the long run because of competition. (The market would be larger than

EXHIBIT III. DECISIONS AND EVENTS FOR STYGIAN CHEMICAL INDUSTRIES, LTD.

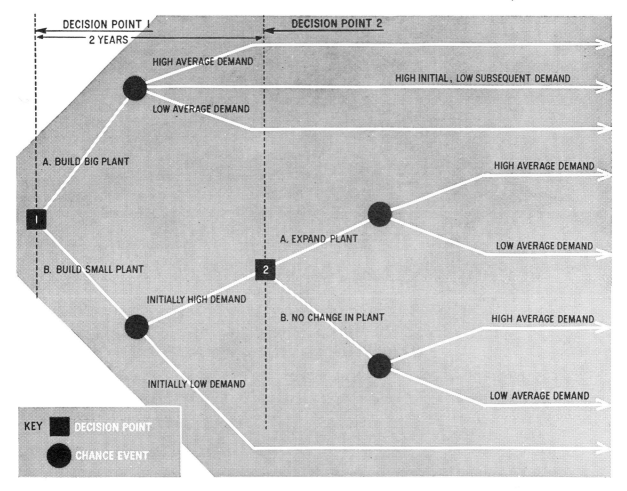

under Alternative 3, but would be divided up among more competitors.)

5. If the small plant were expanded to meet sustained high demand, it would yield $700,000 cash flow annually, and so would be less efficient than a large plant built initially.

6. If the small plant were expanded but high demand were not sustained, estimated annual cash flow would be $50,000.

¶ It is estimated further that a large plant would cost $3 million to put into operation, a small plant would cost $1.3 million, and the expansion of the small plant would cost an additional $2.2 million.

When the foregoing data are incorporated, we have the decision tree shown in EXHIBIT IV. Bear in mind that nothing is shown here which Stygian Chemical's executives did not know before; no numbers have been pulled out of hats. However, we are beginning to see dramatic evidence of the value of decision trees in *laying out*

what management knows in a way that enables more systematic analysis and leads to better decisions. To sum up the requirements of making a decision tree, management must:

1. Identify the points of decision and alternatives available at each point.

2. Identify the points of uncertainty and the type or range of alternative outcomes at each point.

3. Estimate the values needed to make the analysis, especially the probabilities of different events or results of action and the costs and gains of various events and actions.

4. Analyze the alternative values to choose a course.

Choosing Course of Action

We are now ready for the next step in the analysis — to compare the consequences of different courses of action. A decision tree does not give management the answer to an investment problem; rather, it helps management determine which alternative at any particular choice point will yield the greatest expected monetary gain, given the information and alternatives pertinent to the decision.

Of course, the gains must be viewed with the risks. At Stygian Chemical, as at many corporations, managers have different points of view toward risk; hence they will draw different conclusions in the circumstances described by the decision tree shown in Exhibit IV. The many people participating in a decision — those supplying capital, ideas, data, or decisions, and having different values at risk — will see the uncertainty surrounding the decision in different ways. Unless these differences are recognized and dealt with, those who must make the decision, pay for it, supply data and analyses to it, and live with it will judge the issue, relevance of data, need for analysis, and criterion of success in different and conflicting ways.

For example, company stockholders may treat a particular investment as one of a series of pos-

sibilities, some of which will work out, others of which will fail. A major investment may pose risks to a middle manager — to his job and career — no matter what decision is made. Another participant may have a lot to gain from success, but little to lose from failure of the project. The nature of the risk — as each individual sees it — will affect not only the assumptions he is willing to make but also the strategy he will follow in dealing with the risk.

The existence of multiple, unstated, and conflicting objectives will certainly contribute to the "politics" of Stygian Chemical's decision, and one can be certain that the political element exists whenever the lives and ambitions of people are affected. Here, as in similar cases, it is not a bad exercise to think through who the parties to an investment decision are and to try to make these assessments:

• *What is at risk?* Is it profit or equity value, survival of the business, maintenance of a job, opportunity for a major career?

EXHIBIT IV. DECISION TREE WITH FINANCIAL DATA

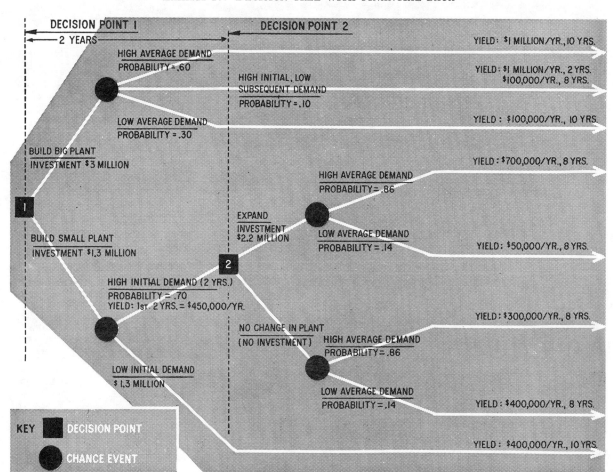

• *Who is bearing the risk?* The stockholder is usually bearing risk in one form. Management, employees, the community — all may be bearing different risks.

• *What is the character of the risk that each person bears?* Is it, *in his terms*, unique, once-in-a-lifetime, sequential, insurable? Does it affect the economy, the industry, the company, or a portion of the company?

Considerations such as the foregoing will surely enter into top management's thinking, and the decision tree in EXHIBIT IV will not eliminate them. But the tree will show management what decision today will contribute most to its long-term goals. The tool for this next step in the analysis is the concept of "rollback."

"Rollback" Concept

Here is how rollback works in the situation described. At the time of making Decision #1 (see EXHIBIT IV), management does not have to make Decision #2 and does not even know if it will have the occasion to do so. But if it *were* to have the option at Decision #2, the company would expand the plant, in view of its current knowledge. The analysis is shown in EXHIBIT V. (I shall ignore for the moment the question of discounting future profits; that is introduced later.) We see that the total expected value of the expansion alternative is $160,000 greater than the no-expansion alternative, over the eight-year life remaining. Hence that is the alternative management would choose if faced with Decision #2 with its existing information (and thinking only of monetary gain as a standard of choice).

Readers may wonder why we started with Decision #2 when today's problem is Decision #1. The reason is the following: We need to be able to put a monetary value on Decision #2 in order to "roll back" to Decision #1 and compare the gain from taking the lower branch ("Build Small Plant") with the gain from taking the upper branch ("Build Big Plant"). Let us call that monetary value for Decision #2 its *position value*. The position value of a decision is the expected value of the preferred branch (in this case, the plant-expan-

sion fork). The expected value is simply a kind of average of the results you would expect if you were to repeat the situation over and over — getting a $5,600 thousand yield 86% of the time and a $400 thousand yield 14% of the time.

Stated in another way, it is worth $2,672 thousand to Stygian Chemical to get to the position where it can make Decision #2. The question is: Given this value and the other data shown in EXHIBIT IV, what now appears to be the best action at Decision #1?

Turn now to EXHIBIT VI. At the right of the branches in the top half we see the yields for various events if a big plant is built (these are simply the figures in EXHIBIT IV multiplied out). In the bottom half we see the small plant figures, including Decision #2 position value plus the yield for the two years prior to Decision #2. If we reduce all these yields by their probabilities, we get the following comparison:

Build big plant: ($10 x .60) + ($2.8 x .10) +
    ($1 x .30) − $3 = $3,600 thousand
Build small plant: ($3.6 x .70) + ($4 x .30) −
    $1.3 = $2,400 thousand

EXHIBIT V. ANALYSIS OF POSSIBLE DECISION #2
(Using maximum expected total cash flow as criterion)

Choice	Chance event	Probability (1)	Total yield, 8 years (thousands of dollars) (2)	Expected value (thousands of dollars) (1) x (2)
Expansion	High average demand	.86	$5,600	$4,816
	Low average demand	.14	400	56
			Total	$4,872
			Less investment	2,200
			Net	$2,672
No Expansion	High average demand	.86	$2,400	$2,064
	Low average demand	.14	3,200	448
			Total	$2,512
			Less investment	0
			Net	$2,512

The choice which maximizes expected total cash yield at Decision #1, therefore, is to build the big plant initially.

Accounting for Time

What about taking differences in the *time* of future earnings into account? The time between successive decision stages on a decision tree may be substantial. At any stage, we may have to weigh differences in immediate cost or revenue against differences in value at the next stage. Whatever standard of choice is applied, we can put the two alternatives on a comparable basis if we discount the value assigned to the next stage by an appropriate percentage. The

at 10%, we get the data shown in Part A of Exhibit VII. Note particularly that these are the present values *as of the time Decision #2 is made.*

Now we want to go through the same procedure used in Exhibit V when we obtained expected values, only this time using the discounted yield figures and obtaining a discount-

EXHIBIT VI. CASH FLOW ANALYSIS FOR DECISION #1

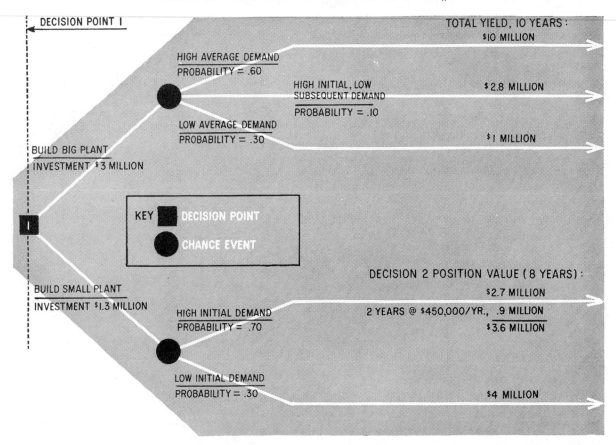

discount percentage is, in effect, an allowance for the cost of capital and is similar to the use of a discount rate in the present value or discounted cash flow techniques already well known to businessmen.

When decision trees are used, the discounting procedure can be applied one stage at a time. Both cash flows and position values are discounted.

For simplicity, let us assume that a discount rate of 10% per year for all stages is decided on by Stygian Chemical's management. Applying the rollback principle, we again begin with Decision #2. Taking the same figures used in previous exhibits and discounting the cash flows

ed expected value. The results are shown in Part B of Exhibit VII. Since the discounted expected value of the no-expansion alternative is higher, *that* figure becomes the position value of Decision #2 this time.

Having done this, we go back to work through Decision #1 again, repeating the same analytical procedure as before only with discounting. The calculations are shown in Exhibit VIII. Note that the Decision #2 position value is treated at the time of Decision #1 as if it were a lump sum received at the end of the two years.

The large-plant alternative is again the preferred one on the basis of discounted expected cash flow. But the margin of difference over

EXHIBIT VII. ANALYSIS OF DECISION #2 WITH DISCOUNTING

A. Present values of cash flows

Choice — outcome	Yield	Present value (in thousands)
Expand — high demand	$700,000/year, 8 years	$4,100
Expand — low demand	50,000/year, 8 years	300
No change — high demand	300,000/year, 8 years	1,800
No change — low demand	400,000/year, 8 years	2,300

B. Obtaining discounted expected values

Choice	Chance event	Probability (1)	Present value yield (in thousands) (2)	Discounted expected value (in thousands) (1) x (2)
Expansion	High average demand	.86	$4,100	$3,526
	Low average demand	.14	300	42
			Total	$3,568
			Less investment	2,200
			Net	$1,368
No expansion	High average demand	.86	$1,800	$1,548
	Low average demand	.14	2,300	322
			Total	$1,870
			Less investment	0
			Net	$1,870

NOTE: For simplicity, the first year cash flow is not discounted, the second year cash flow is discounted one year, and so on.

EXHIBIT VIII. ANALYSIS OF DECISION #1

Choice	Chance event	Proba- bility (1)	Yield (in thousands)	Discounted value of yield (in thousands) (2)	Discounted expected yield (in thousands) (1) x (2)
Build big plant	High average demand	.60	$1,000/year, 10 years	$6,700	$4,020
	High initial, low average demand	.10	1,000/year, 2 years 100/year, 8 years	2,400	240
	Low average demand	.30	100/year, 10 years	700	210
				Total	$4,470
				Less investment	3,000
				Net	$1,470
Build small plant	High initial demand	.70	$ 450/year, 2 years	$ 860	$ 600
			Decision #2 value, $1,870 at end of 2 years	1,530	1,070
	Low initial demand	.30	$ 400/year, 10 years	2,690	810
				Total	$2,480
				Less investment	1,300
				Net	$1,180

the small-plant alternative ($290 thousand) is smaller than it was without discounting.

Uncertainty Alternatives

In illustrating the decision-tree concept, I have treated uncertainty alternatives as if they were discrete, well-defined possibilities. For my examples I have made use of uncertain situations depending basically on a single variable, such as the level of demand or the success or failure of a development project. I have sought to avoid unnecessary complication while putting emphasis on the key interrelationships among the present decision, future choices, and the intervening uncertainties.

In many cases, the uncertain elements do take the form of discrete, single-variable alternatives. In others, however, the possibilities for cash flow during a stage may range through a whole spectrum and may depend on a number of independent or partially related variables subject to chance influences — cost, demand, yield, economic climate, and so forth. In these cases, we have found that the range of variability or the likelihood of the cash flow falling in a given range during a stage can be calculated readily from knowledge of the key variables and the uncertainties surrounding them. Then the range of cash-flow possibilities during the stage can be broken down into two, three, or more "subsets," which can be used as discrete chance alternatives.

Conclusion

Peter F. Drucker has succinctly expressed the relation between present planning and future events: "Long-range planning does not deal with future decisions. It deals with the futurity of present decisions." [2] Today's decision should be made in light of the anticipated effect it and the outcome of uncertain events will have on future values and decisions. Since today's decision sets the stage for tomorrow's decision, today's decision must balance economy with flexibility; it must balance the need to capitalize on profit opportunities that may exist with the capacity to react to future circumstances and needs.

The unique feature of the decision tree is that it allows management to combine analytical techniques such as discounted cash flow and present value methods with a clear portrayal of the impact of future decision alternatives and events. Using the decision tree, management can consider various courses of action with greater ease and clarity. The interactions between present decision alternatives, uncertain events, and future choices and their results become more visible.

Of course, there are many practical aspects of decision trees in addition to those that could be covered in the space of just one article. When these other aspects are discussed in subsequent articles, the whole range of possible gains for management will be seen in greater detail.

Surely the decision-tree concept does not offer final answers to managements making investment decisions in the face of uncertainty. We have not reached that stage, and perhaps we never will. Nevertheless, the concept is valuable for illustrating the structure of investment decisions, and it can likewise provide excellent help in the evaluation of capital investment *opportunities*.

APPENDIX

For readers interested in further examples of decision-tree structure, I shall describe in this appendix two representative situations with which I am familiar and show the trees that might be drawn to analyze management's decision-making alternatives. We shall not concern ourselves here with costs, yields, probabilities, or expected values.

New Facility

The choice of alternatives in building a plant depends upon market forecasts. The alternative

chosen will, in turn, affect the market outcome. For example, the military products division of a diversified firm, after some period of low profits due to intense competition, has won a contract to produce a new type of military engine suitable for Army transport vehicles. The division has a contract to build productive capacity and to produce at a specified contract level over a period of three years.

FIGURE A illustrates the situation. The dotted line shows the contract rate. The solid line shows the proposed buildup of production for the military. Some other possibilities are portrayed by

[2] "Long-Range Planning," *Management Science*, April 1959, p. 239.

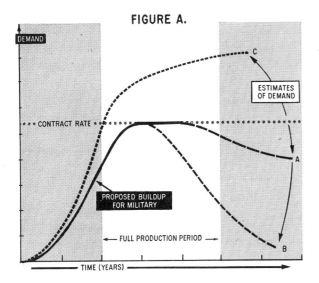

FIGURE A.

dashed lines. The company is not sure whether the contract will be continued at a relatively high rate after the third year, as shown by Line A, or whether the military will turn to another newer development, as indicated by Line B. The company has no guarantee of compensation after the third year. There is also the possibility, indicated by Line C, of a large additional commercial market for the product, this possibility being somewhat dependent on the cost at which the product can be made and sold.

If this commercial market could be tapped, it would represent a major new business for the company and a substantial improvement in the profitability of the division and its importance to the company.

Management wants to explore three ways of producing the product as follows:

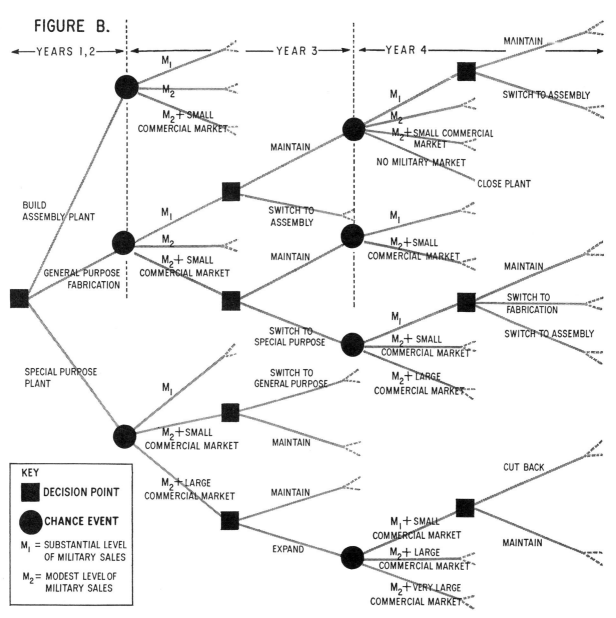

FIGURE B.

(1) It might subcontract all fabrication and set up a simple assembly with limited need for investment in plant and equipment; the costs would tend to be relatively high and the company's investment and profit opportunity would be limited, but the company assets which are at risk would also be limited.

(2) It might undertake the major part of the fabrication itself but use general-purpose machine tools in a plant of general-purpose construction. The division would have a chance to retain more of the most profitable operations itself, exploiting some technical developments it has made (on the basis of which it got the contract). While the cost of production would still be relatively high, the nature of the investment in plant and equipment would be such that it could probably be turned to other uses or liquidated if the business disappeared.

(3) The company could build a highly mechanized plant with specialized fabrication and assembly equipment, entailing the largest investment but yielding a substantially lower unit manufacturing cost if manufacturing volume were adequate. Following this plan would improve the chances for a continuation of the military contract and penetration into the commercial market and would improve the profitability of whatever business might be obtained in these markets. Failure to sustain either the military or the commercial market, however, would cause substantial financial loss.

Either of the first two alternatives would be better adapted to low-volume production than would the third.

Some major uncertainties are: the cost-volume relationships under the alternative manufacturing methods; the size and structure of the future market — this depends in part on cost, but the degree and extent of dependence are unknown; and the possibilities of competitive developments which would render the product competitively or technologically obsolete.

How would this situation be shown in decision-tree form? (Before going further you might want to draw a tree for the problem yourself.) FIGURE B shows my version of a tree. Note that in this case the chance alternatives are somewhat influenced by the decision made. A decision, for example, to build a more efficient plant will open possibilities for an expanded market.

Plant Modernization

A company management is faced with a decision on a proposal by its engineering staff which, after three years of study, wants to install a computer-based control system in the company's major plant. The expected cost of the control system is some $30 million. The claimed advantages of the system will be a reduction in labor cost and an improved product yield. These benefits depend on the level of product throughput, which is likely to rise over the next decade. It is thought that the installation program will take about two years and will cost a substantial amount over and above the cost of equipment. The engineers calculate that the automation project will yield a 20% return on investment, after taxes; the projection is based on a ten-year forecast of product demand by the market research department, and an assumption of an eight-year life for the process control system.

What would this investment yield? Will actual product sales be higher or lower than forecast? Will the process work? Will it achieve the economies expected? Will competitors follow if the com-

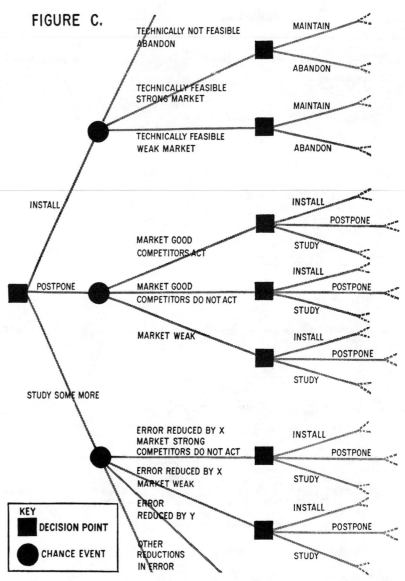

FIGURE C.

KEY

■ DECISION POINT

● CHANCE EVENT

pany is successful? Are they going to mechanize anyway? Will new products or processes make the basic plant obsolete before the investment can be recovered? Will the controls last eight years? Will something better come along sooner?

The initial decision alternatives are (a) to install the proposed control system, (b) postpone action until trends in the market and/or competition become clearer, or (c) initiate more investigation or an independent evaluation. Each alternative will be followed by resolution of some uncertain aspect, in part dependent on the action taken. This resolution will lead in turn to a new decision. The

dotted lines at the right of FIGURE C indicate that the decision tree continues indefinitely, though the decision alternatives do tend to become repetitive. In the case of postponement or further study, the decisions are to install, postpone, or restudy; in the case of installation, the decisions are to continue operation or abandon.

An immediate decision is often one of a sequence. It may be one of a number of sequences. The impact of the present decision in narrowing down future alternatives and the effect of future alternatives in affecting the value of the present choice must both be considered.

Reprint 64410

Decision analysis comes of age

No longer the exclusive toy of management scientists, decision analysis is becoming an accepted managerial tool for solving everyday business problems

Jacob W. Ulvila and Rex V. Brown

Ten years ago, decision analysis was still an experimental management technique. But even then supporters claimed that eventually it would become for the manager what calculus is to the engineer. According to the authors of this article, decision analysis that incorporates personal judgment has not yet become what some expected, but it has, nonetheless, gained acceptance in many large corporations and government departments. One of the reasons for this acceptance is the greater flexibility and sensitivity of decision analysis to managers' needs than earlier forms had. In other words, today's decision analysis techniques can better take into account the people, the politics, the time pressures, and all the messy but critical factors that managers have to contend with. In this article, the authors describe three major forms of decision analysis and show how real managers have used decision tree analysis, probabilistic forecasting, and multiattribute analysis to solve real business problems.

Mr. Ulvila is vice president of Decision Science Consortium, Inc., a management consulting firm based in Falls Church, Virginia. He specializes in the application of decision analysis and other quantitative methods to a variety of problem areas, especially business planning. Mr. Brown is chairman of the board of Decision Science Consortium, Inc. Formerly on the faculty of Harvard Business School, he is author or coauthor of four books on decision analysis and marketing, including Decision Analysis for the Manager (New York: Holt, Rinehart & Winston, 1974). This is his second article in HBR.

In the early 1970s, C. Jackson Grayson, onetime head of the Wage and Price Commission and also author of one of the first books on applied decision analysis, urged analysts to "put people, time, power, data accessibility, and response time into models and create crude, workable solutions" if they wanted busy people like himself to use them.[1]

At the time, decision analysis was still an experimental management technique, a fairly straightforward application of statistical decision theory.[2] The choice facing a decision maker was expressed as a mathematical function of probability and utility numbers, which measured the person's uncertainties and value judgments. (The best option was the one with the highest expected utility.) Although decision analysis was well established as a way to quantify logically the considerations that go into any choice among options, it had just begun to move out of the business schools and into practical application in the business world. Only a handful of corporations provided in-house expertise, and consultants specializing in decision analysis were rarely called on.

Now, after ten years of sometimes humbling feedback from the real world, analysts have learned to be more flexible and modest in how to make the basic decision theory formulation useful to managers. The technology has been enhanced to capture more considerations relevant to sound decision making, notably through multiattribute utility analysis and improved interaction with the user. Decision analysis has emerged as a complement to older decision-making techniques such as systems modeling and operations research. In addition to statistical decision theory, the new technology draws on psychology, economics, and social science.

Editor's note: All references are listed at the end of the article on page 14.

What is retained and is distinctive about the approach is that the quantitative models incorporate personal judgments. To distinguish this approach from other ways of analyzing decisions in widespread use (such as those that depend only on "objective" inputs), we call it personalized decision analysis.

Analysts have learned to use the data and expertise that are immediately available to the decision maker and to play back conclusions to the manager in close to real time. In 1970, an analysis was rarely completed within three months. Now, meaningful analysis of a problem can be generated in an afternoon, and a succession of analyses can be presented in intervals of one or two days. Without greatly disturbing their schedule of meetings or reflective process, managers can now respond to these analyses and provide input for other rounds.

Although such decision analysis has not become the dominant analytic discipline that some people expected, its use has grown dramatically since 1970. Personalized decision analysis has become an accepted part of the staff services that major corporations draw on routinely, much as they do industrial psychology, cost analysis, marketing research, and economic analysis. And virtually all the major areas of government have adopted decision analysis in one form or another.

The case studies that we present in this article illustrate how managers use the three major variants of decision analysis currently in use—decision tree analysis, probabilistic forecasting, and multiattribute utility analysis.

Decision tree analysis

Decision tree analysis is the oldest and most widely used form of decision analysis. Managers have used it in making business decisions in uncertain conditions since the late 1950s, and its techniques are familiar.[3] Over the past several years, however, the manner in which people conduct decision tree analysis has expanded. Today's analyst has at his or her disposal not only an array of computer supports that make quick turnaround possible but also the accumulated wisdom of analysts over the last 20 years. The following case illustrates some of the components of a successful decision tree analysis. They include the use of simple displays, sensitivity analysis to guide refinements, and subsidiary models to ensure completeness. Also important are the direction and integration the analysis gives to the contributions of experts as well as the involvement of top managers.

Should AIL purchase rights to a new patent?

Late in 1974, the AIL Division of Cutler-Hammer, Inc. (now a division of Eaton Corporation) was offered the opportunity to acquire the defense market rights to a new flight-safety system patent. The inventor claimed he had a strong patent position as well as technical superiority, but the market for the product was very uncertain, mostly because of pending legislative action. Because the inventor wished to make an offer to other companies if AIL was not interested, he asked AIL to make the decision in a few weeks, a period of time clearly inadequate to resolve any uncertainties it was aware of.

AIL had not used formal decision analysis before. Top managers were, however, familiar with the theory and its typical applications through the literature and interested in trying these techniques on an actual decision to evaluate their worth. The patent decision appeared to be a good candidate for such a trial.

A team of AIL personnel and outside analysts spent two weeks developing an analysis of the patent idea. All the while, the team stayed in continual contact with top management.

AIL's analysis
The analysts used standard decision tree techniques. *Exhibit I* shows the immediate choice, to purchase a six-month option on the patent rights or not, and the main uncertainties that affected the decision. The attractiveness of each outcome, or path through the tree, is represented by its present-value earnings. These range from a loss of $700,000 to a gain of $10.5 million. The expected value at each node in the tree is calculated by taking a probability-weighted average of its branches. Working these values gives an expected value of $100,425. That is, AIL could expect to be better off by $100,425 if it purchased the six-month option.

The mechanics of the analysis—specifying the tree, assigning values, and calculating results—are straightforward. The usefulness of the analysis, however, depends more on how the analysis process is managed than on the mechanics. Five features that are often absent in unsuccessful attempts to apply decision analysis marked this implementation as a success.

A simple display. The focus of the analysis was the simple tree shown in *Exhibit I*. The most common mistake that a beginner at decision analysis makes is to include everything the choice involves in the tree. This is a sure way to end up with a mess, which only the analyst, if anyone, can under-

Exhibit I   **AIL's decision tree**

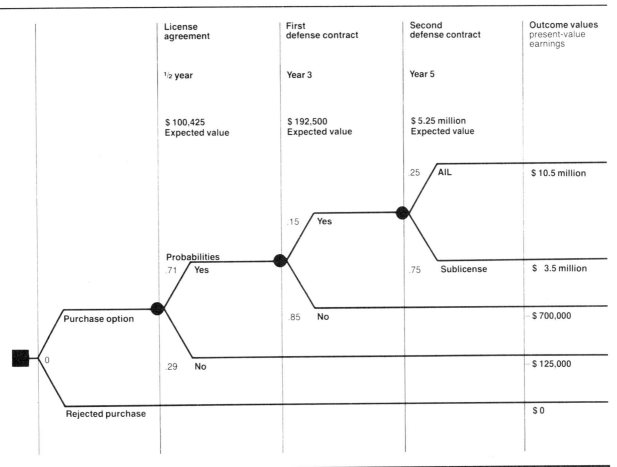

License agreement	First defense contract	Second defense contract	Outcome values present-value earnings
¹/₂ year	Year 3	Year 5	
$ 100,425 Expected value	$ 192,500 Expected value	$ 5.25 million Expected value	

.25 AIL $ 10.5 million

.15 Yes

Probabilities
.71 Yes   .75 Sublicense $ 3.5 million

Purchase option

.85 No   — $ 700,000

0

.29 No   — $ 125,000

Rejected purchase $ 0

Exhibit II   **Risk profiles for AIL's patent purchasing decision**
distribution of incremental discounted earnings in millions of dollars

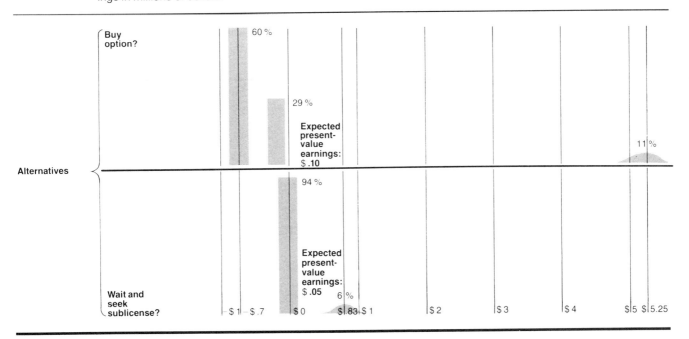

Buy option?

60 %

29 %

Expected present-value earnings: $ .10

11 %

Alternatives

94 %

Expected present-value earnings: $ .05

6 %

Wait and seek sublicense?

— $ 1 — $ .7 $ 0 $.83 $ 1 $ 2 $ 3 $ 4 $ 5 $ 5.25

stand. Such a tree is unlikely to influence any manager's decision.

The trick is to design a simple tree that captures the essence of the problem by including its most important elements. In this case, the most important elements affecting earnings were the probabilities of exercising the option, receiving an initial contract, and continuing on a second contract.

Refining the elements. By means of an interactive computer program, the analysts determined how sensitive the results were to changes in the inputs to the tree. The analysis was then expanded in a way that would be most responsive to what the decision maker needed to know.

Use of subsidiary models. The analysts at AIL developed models to refine estimates of the most sensitive inputs. Using a simple tree does not make the analysis coarse or incomplete; subsidiary models can ensure any desired level of detail and sophistication. In this case, the analysts used three subsidiary models. They used one to determine yearly earnings and calculate present values and another to assess the probability of receiving a contract.

The latter model reflected important factors such as the timing and terms of a possible legislative mandate for the system, the strength of possible competitive systems, and the likelihood of a crash or near crash of a plane within the next several months. The analysts used a third model to assess probability distributions of earnings from the contracts that reflected uncertainties in the number of units, the price per unit, and the profit margin. Each subsidiary model was compact and could be displayed on a single chart, which the analysts used to answer top managers' questions about how the figures in the main model had been determined.

Team input. At AIL various people were involved with each aspect of the model, so that each expert could focus on the area of his expertise. Those most knowledgeable about the chances of winning the second contract, for example, addressed this aspect of the problem but did not consider other aspects. The combined contributions of all the experts formed a unified picture for top management.

Contact with top management. The most important factor was the close work of top management with the analysis team throughout the analysis. This interaction ensured that:

1   The choices modeled were in fact the choices under consideration. (In this case, as a result of the modeling, the analysts identified a new choice — waiting and seeking a sublicense.)

2   All important concerns were addressed. For AIL, the issues included the impact that decision factors other than direct earnings have (in this case, return on capital).

3   The level of modeling was right. That is, some aspects were modeled formally, but others were left to informal consideration. For example, the analysts explored AIL's attitude toward risk taking by displaying risk profiles of the choices rather than by assessing and using a utility function.[4] (Because answering the hypothetical questions about preferences for uncertain returns that are required to establish a utility function strikes many managers as gambling, many of them are reluctant to do it. In this case, the uncertainties of the decision could be sufficiently characterized in simple risk profiles.)

Exhibit II shows the risk profiles of the alternatives AIL faced. Purchasing the option would give an expected net present value of earnings of about $100,000, a 60% chance of losing about $700,000, a 29% chance of losing about $125,000, and an 11% chance of having a positive return from a distribution with an expectation of about $5.25 million. (This picture corresponds to a more detailed analysis of the earnings from a defense contract.)

The alternative, waiting and seeking a sublicense, would have a 94% chance of producing no gain (or loss) and a 6% chance of producing a distribution with an expectation of about $830,000 and would result in an expected value of about $50,000. This display facilitated a unanimous decision by the decision-making group (the president and his vice presidents for business development and operations) to go with the less risky strategy even though it offered a slightly lower expected value.

Other companies' experiences

Companies in a wide range of industries are using decision tree analysis to make a variety of decisions. For example:

☐   Through this kind of analysis, Ford has determined whether to produce its own tires and whether to stop producing convertibles.

☐   The defense systems division of Honeywell uses decision tree analysis to evaluate the attractiveness of new weapons programs. On a regular basis, program managers and the director of planning develop models to help decide which programs to pursue and how they should allocate internal research and development funds.

☐   With decision tree analysis, Pillsbury's grocery products division has evaluated major decisions, such as whether to switch from a box to a bag for a certain grocery product. In this case, even when analysts used pessimistic assessments expressed by a manager who initially recommended remaining with the box, the analysis showed that the profitability would be greater with the bag. The analysis also showed that the value of making a market test, as urged by some executives, could not remotely approach its cost. The bag was introduced, and the profits on the product climbed.

☐   Faced with a decision to electrify part of its system, which would involve capital expenditures of several hundred million dollars, Southern Railway carried out an analysis that gave managers a better understanding of the interactions of variables influencing the decision.

☐   Many major oil and gas companies, such as Union Texas Petroleum, the Champlin oil and gas subsidiary of Union Pacific, and Gulf Oil, apply decision analysis regularly to choose appropriate sites for exploration and evaluate the economics of field development.

☐   ITT uses decision analysis at many levels of the company, especially for capital investment decisions.

Probabilistic forecasting

The previous section illustrates how personalized decision analysis can capture all the thinking that goes into a particular decision. The technique has other uses as well. Analysts can develop certain aspects of decision analysis into analytic tools that can be used in a variety of contexts. Analysts can use the probabilistic modeling aspects of decision analysis to develop forecasts of, for instance, future sales and profits, which in turn can be used to support decisions about planning, investment, and marketing. Developing a single aspect of personalized decision analysis to support decisions in a variety of contexts is likely to become very popular. Because its cost can be spread over many uses, a company can afford to use enough computerization and staff time to do this type of analysis properly.

The following example illustrates how personalized decision analysis can be used for forecasting. Of course, this kind of analysis is not the only way to carry out quantitative forecasting. What is distinctive about this approach's contribution to the problem is that, rather than limit a forecast to statistical extrapolation from the past, it can combine assessments of judgment with data. In cases where little or no relevant history is available on which to base a forecast and where each product's success depends on a combination of events about which personal judgment is virtually the only source of information, this form of analysis is particularly helpful.

How will Honeywell's defense division grow?

In late 1979, the manager of planning for the defense systems division of Honeywell, Inc. faced the task of planning the division's growth over the next ten years. A major part of the work involved finding how to stay within the R&D budget and yet pursue new product opportunities to increase the division's sales and profits.

After he screened the new product opportunities according to their fit with the rest of the division, the manager needed forecasts of the products' sales, profits, and investment requirements. The products' successful development, the strength of competition, and their eventual market success were all uncertain. In addition, the chances for success of some of the products were interrelated, and several products offered the chance of significant collateral business.

The approach the analysts took was to build a composite forecast for the division by combining decision tree analyses of individual products. During the project, Honeywell's planners worked closely with decision analysis consultants and, by the time they had finished, had acquired the skills needed to carry out the analyses in-house. This type of analysis is now a regular part of Honeywell's project evaluation, planning, and forecasting activity.

The analysts developed a model for each product along lines similar to AIL's. The analysis team worked closely with each project manager and his staff to build the decision tree, assess probabilities and values, and discuss results and sensitivities.

The two analyses differed significantly, however, in a number of ways. First, the results of Honeywell's analysis were to be used for forecasting as well as for decision making. This use meant that the analysts would need to model additional factors and would have to make the form the outputs took suitable for forecasting.

Second, because the success of some products was related to the the success of others, the analysts had to include in the analysis such factors as common investments, collateral business opportunities, and marketing interactions.

Third, Honeywell's problem presented no clear single criterion according to which management could make a decision. Honeywell considered several financial criteria such as internal rate of return, net present value, and yearly streams of profits, investments, and return on investment.

Honeywell's forecasts
Exhibit III shows the probabilistic sales forecast for one group of interrelated products. This

Exhibit III   **Distribution of sales for a group of interrelated products**

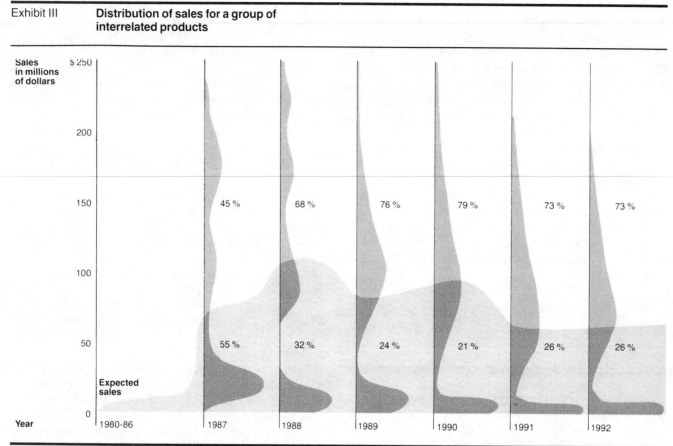

Sales in millions of dollars

$250

200

150   45 %   68 %   76 %   79 %   73 %   73 %

100

50   55 %   32 %   24 %   21 %   26 %   26 %

Expected sales

0

Year   1980-86   1987   1988   1989   1990   1991   1992

Exhibit IV   **Detailed forecast of sales in 1988**

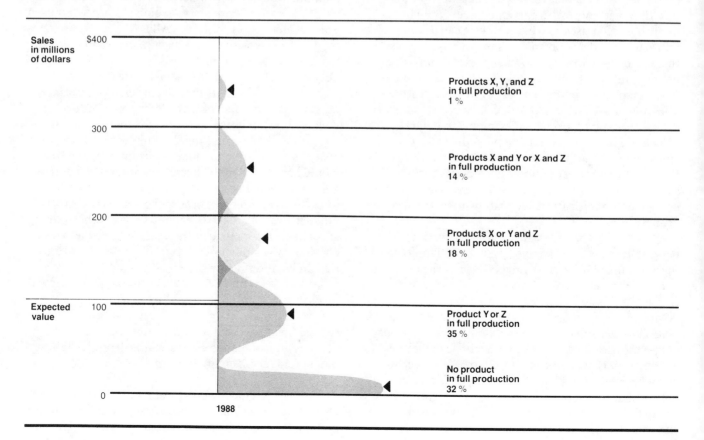

Sales in millions of dollars

$400

Products X, Y, and Z
in full production
1 %

300

Products X and Y or X and Z
in full production
14 %

200

Products X or Y and Z
in full production
18 %

Expected value   100

Product Y or Z
in full production
35 %

No product
in full production
32 %

0

1988

forecast is based on decision tree analyses of three main products and two collateral business opportunities. The analysts first developed decision trees for each product to determine the distributions of sales in the event that a market sufficient to support full production both did and did not emerge. Then they developed a second level of analysis to model the key interdependencies among the products; specifically, the probability of any particular product being in full production depended on which other products were also in full production.

The forecast shows that low sales are expected from the products for the first seven years. After that, sales for the next six years are expected to be about $75 million per year. This amount is not certain, however. The forecast, for instance, shows a 24% chance of sales being below $25 million in 1989.

The supporting decision tree analyses were useful for explaining the shape of each year's forecast. *Exhibit IV* shows that because of uncertainty about which products would have sufficient markets to support full production by 1988, the forecast for sales is "lumpy." The reasons for these uncertainties are detailed in the decision tree analyses.

This analysis helped Honeywell to assess the chances that these products would meet sales goals, the uncertainties in the assessment, and the reasons for the uncertainties. By detailing the chain of events that would produce different levels of sales, it also identified points of leverage – places where Honeywell could take action to change probabilities and improve sales.

The analysts also used the decision trees to forecast yearly profits, fund flows, assets, research and development investments, and the related financial quantities of net present value, internal rate of return, and annual return on investment. Their forecasts indicated that these products could be expected to exceed requirements on all factors and that, unless Honeywell was very risk averse, they were attractive.

Honeywell's managers compared forecasts to decide which product opportunities to pursue. These comparisons provided an additional screen since some products were clearly worse than others on *all* factors. But because the analysis didn't show the relative importance of each factor – some products were projected to perform better on certain factors (for example, internal rate of return and net present value) and other products were projected to perform better on other factors (for example, return on investment) – an unambiguous ordering of the products was impossible. Honeywell's managers might have had such an ordering if their analysts had used some of the newer techniques of multiattribute utility.

Multiattribute utility analysis

In trying to determine where to place its European subsidiary, the top management of one company completely ignored a decision tree analysis that showed careful consideration of the financial implications of possible locations. When pressed for an explanation, top management confided that the choice was dominated by the fact that key personnel wanted to be near the International School in Geneva. Somehow, that consideration seemed too noneconomical and nonrational to be included in the analysis – yet it did dominate the decision. At the time the decision was made, the technology of decision analysis was ill equipped to handle the trade-offs between financial effects and intangibles. A new technique, multiattribute utility analysis, makes such modeling possible by precisely specifying the factors that affect the choice, making trade-offs among the factors, and choosing the alternative that offers the best balance.

Multiattribute utility analysis evolved out of decision analysis that supported government decisions, in which the need to balance multiple objectives is most obvious. As the case of the company deciding where to put its plant shows, however, its usefulness for business decision making is evident. For example, plant sites usually differ in such intangibles as the skill of the local work force, the ability of local management, and the management problems of operating plants in the locations under consideration. These are important factors to consider in the decision of where to locate the plant, yet it is virtually impossible to specify their impact on profit with any precision.

Many factors also arise in strategic decisions. For example, Michael E. Porter has argued that, when considering the strategic decisions of vertical integration, major capacity expansion, and entry into new businesses, managers should go beyond cost and investment analyses to consider broad strategic issues and perplexing administrative problems and that these are very hard to quantify.[5] Multiattribute utility analysis, which is illustrated in the following case, provides a way to quantify and trade off such factors.

Which bomb detection system should the FAA choose?

Over the past few years, the Federal Aviation Administration has been supporting research and development on a system to detect bombs in airplane

Exhibit V **Hierarchy of attributes in the FAA's analysis**
in preference weights

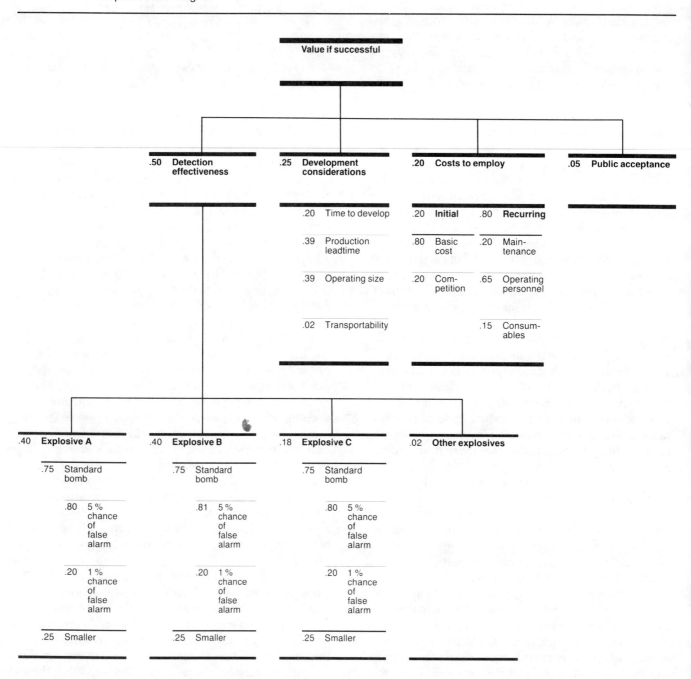

baggage. In early 1980, the program manager for this project had to decide which of several candidate systems to continue funding. The candidates differed greatly in their potential performance and technical characteristics. Since none was clearly superior in all respects, the program manager sought a method for weighing the various characteristics to arrive at a measure of overall value.

A team of outside analysts worked closely with the program manager and other FAA per-

sonnel to develop a comprehensive model of the value of each system. To determine an efficient allocation of budgeted funds, they combined these values with assessments of the probabilities of success and development costs.

The FAA's analysis

The analysts' primary goal was to develop a comprehensive model for evaluating and comparing candidates. This development involved four activities—defining attributes of value, assessing performance of the candidates on each attribute, determining trade-offs across attributes, and calculating overall values.[6]

Defining preference attributes. The analysts sought to define attributes with four characteristics. The attributes were to be comprehensive enough to account for most of what is important in evaluating the candidates, to highlight the differences among the candidates, to reflect separate, nonoverlapping values to avoid double counting, and to be independent of each other.

When the analysts had identified attributes that satisfied these four requirements, they then arranged the attributes in a hierarchy showing the logical relationships among attributes. This is shown in *Exhibit V.*

The first main attribute is the effectiveness of the device at detecting bombs. This is subdivided into the type of explosive, the size of the bomb, and the detection-false alarm ratio.

The second main attribute, development considerations, is divided into four subcategories—time to develop a prototype, production lead time, operating size (which would determine a system's location in an airport), and transportability.

Cost to employ the system in an airport, the third main attribute, is divided into initial costs and recurring costs. Initial costs reflect a basic cost estimate based on technical considerations and an estimate of the effects of competition. Recurring costs include maintenance, operating personnel, and material consumed during operation.

The fourth main attribute is the system's acceptability to passengers.

Assessing performance of candidates on each attribute. To assess preference, the analysts required scales for all attributes. They used two types of measure—scales with natural standard units (including dollars for costs, months or hours for time, and percentages for detection rates) and relative scales. Wherever possible, the performance of a candidate was first assessed in natural units. These assessments were then transformed into 0-to-100-point scales for standardization. The candidate with the best performance (the lowest cost, for example) received a score of 100; the one with the worst performance (the highest cost, for instance) received a score of 0; and the others received intermediate scores.

Where no natural measure existed (for example, for "public acceptance"), performance was assessed directly on a 0-to-100-point scale. Again, a score of 100 was assigned to the candidate with the best performance, 0 to the worst performance, and so forth.

| Exhibit VI | Performance of the FAA's bomb detection candidates on development considerations on a scale of 0 to 100 |

| Development considerations | Candidates | | | | | |
	A	B	C	D	E	F
Time to develop	100	50	0	62	50	25
Production leadtime	50	100	75	50	0	50
Operating size	100	100	50	100	0	100
Transportability	100	100	100	100	0	60

Exhibit VI shows, for instance, the scores for the six candidates on each development consideration. Candidate A was assessed to have the best "time to develop" since it was fully developed at the time of the analysis. It was assigned a value of 100. Candidate C would take the longest time to develop—four years. It received a value of 0. Other candidates would take intermediate amounts of time to develop and thus received intermediate scores.

Determining trade-offs across attributes. By assessing a set of weights to represent the decision maker's judgment about the relative importance of improving performance from the worst to the best level for each attribute, analysts could determine trade-offs across attributes. The analysts assessed the weights by referring to the range of performance the scales reflected instead of to abstract notions of importance.

Consider, for example, the weights of the development considerations shown in *Exhibit V.* For these attributes, the ranges of possible variation in "production lead time" (18 months) and in "operating size" were considered most important. The variation of "time to develop" (4 years) was assessed to be half as important (as important as a variation of 9 months on "production lead time"). Finally, the variation of "transportability" (32 hours) was assessed to be one-tenth as important as "time to develop" (or about as important as 5 months of development time). These assessments are represented by weights that are in the ratios of .5:1:1:.05 for time to develop, production lead time, operating size, and transportability. Normalized weights of .20:.39:.39:.02 (which retain these ratios) were used for standardization.

The analysts assessed weights both directly, as we explained earlier, and indirectly. They used an indirect method to assess the weight between initial and recurring costs. This method determined weights that were consistent with a 10% discount rate and a ten-year operating horizon.

Calculating overall values. The fourth modeling activity was to calculate a weighted-average score for each candidate by working up through the hierarchy. Thus, using the values in *Exhibit VI* and the weights in *Exhibit V*, analysts calculated the value of candidate A on "development considerations" as:

$$(100)(.20)+(50)(.39)+(100)(.39)+(100)(.02) \simeq 80.$$

Similar calculations produced the values for the candidates on each main attribute that are shown in *Exhibit VII*. The analysts next calculated the overall value of each candidate by taking a weighted average of these scores. For example, the overall value of candidate A is:

$$(57)(.50)+(80)(.25)+(82)(.20)+(70)(.05) \simeq 68.$$

Overall value is a measure of the attractiveness of each candidate that can be compared with measures for other candidates. The result of the analysis shows that candidate B offers the best balance of characteristics, that candidates C and D are almost as attractive, and that candidates E and F offer the worst balances.

The value of the analysis
The FAA's primary use of the analysis was to quantify each candidate's value in a way that permitted comparison. To determine an efficient allocation of R&D funds, the analysts combined these evaluations with estimates of each candidate's probability of success and cost of development.

The FAA's analysis also facilitated several aspects of the decision-making process. First, it helped resolve disagreements. The disaggregation of the elements of the decision clarified the source of a disagreement—was it about facts (for example, the cost of a system) or a difference in judgment (for instance, the relative importance of cost in comparison with detection performance)? Once the disagreements were clear, managers could deal with them by, for example, gathering additional supporting information. If the disagreement persisted, the model could determine its importance. For each input, the model could show whether the disagreement significantly affected the overall evaluation. Even if a disagreement was significant, the model at least isolated its cause. This clarification enabled the ultimate decision maker to make a better judgment.

The disaggregation also allowed the analyst to make a comprehensive analysis of the candidates. The team could investigate each attribute thoroughly yet keep its contribution to the overall evaluation in perspective. This arrangement prevented the analysts from wasting attention on unimportant issues.

To give a balanced picture of the whole, the multiattribute analysis synthesized the various pieces of the assessment. The analysts considered the impact of all important factors before they came up with a recommendation.

Business use of multiattribute utility analysis

Multiattribute utility analysis has been used widely to aid government decision makers. For instance, it has been used to select military systems, set water-supply policy, site nuclear facilities, allocate nuclear inspection resources, determine fire department operations, evaluate crime-prevention programs, and prepare international negotiators.

Its use as an aid in making business decisions has not been as widespread, but the next few years should see a dramatic increase. Multiattribute analysis is useful for any decision in which multiple factors are important, no alternative is clearly best on all factors, and some factors are difficult to quantify. Several business decisions have these characteristics:

Where to put a plant. Sites often differ in many important aspects. Some factors, such as differences in capital costs (land, plant, and equipment) and in operating revenue and expenses (access to markets, labor rates, tax benefits, shipping costs), are easily reduced to financial terms. Other factors that may be crucial to the decision are more difficult to reduce to dollars. These include the availability and skill of local labor, the degree of unionization, the difficulty of managing geographically dispersed units, and legal restrictions on operations. Multiattribute analysis can highlight the sources of differences and enable managers to make quantitative trade-offs between financial factors and "intangibles."

Whether to integrate vertically. A decision to integrate an operation or not requires that management consider a multitude of factors, many of which are difficult to quantify with standard financial techniques: access to new information, access to new technologies, ability to control specifications of products or raw materials, economies of combined operations, difficulty in balancing "upstream" and "downstream" units, and increased fixed costs of doing business.

Whether and how to enter a new business. This decision can involve considerations that are often ignored in capital budgeting:

The production or marketing "fit" between new and existing businesses or technologies.

Exhibit VII **Overall value of candidates**
on a scale of 0 to 100

		Candidates					
Attribute category	Preference weight	A	B	C	D	E	F
Detection effectiveness	.50	57	72	88	62	39	0
Other development considerations	.25	80	90	51	73	10	65
Costs to employ	.20	82	91	88	87	39	70
Public acceptance	.05	70	90	90	85	0	100
	Overall value	68	81	79	71	30	35

Special skills or technologies required to operate the new business.

"Cultural fit" between new and old businesses (especially important if entry is by acquisition).

Relative strengths of competitors in the new business.

By using multiattribute utility analysis, managers can balance these factors against financial considerations to derive a comprehensive evaluation of alternatives.

What and whether to negotiate. Many negotiations—labor, real estate, and sales, for example—may involve several issues. A labor negotiation could include issues of wage rates, length of agreement, grievance procedures, work rules, seniority, job security, union security, vacations, fringe benefits, and pension fund contributions. Both sides' opening positions on the issues are often clear, but how they view the trade-offs across issues is not. Using multiattribute analyses of their own preferences and trade-offs and those of the other side, negotiators can uncover opportunities to give a small concession in return for a large benefit.[7]

How to allocate research and development budgets. Research and development projects often exhibit a variety of performance characteristics that managers may need to balance to determine the best project. Multiattribute utility analysis can help them do this. They can also combine such an analysis with a decision tree analysis to address uncertainties and risks.

The forecast for decision analysis

If the trends of the past decade continue at their present rate, then over the next decade we can certainly expect to see personalized decision analysis spread and become firmly established as a staff function throughout industry. Virtually all corporations of any substance will have in-house staffs or outside consultants to analyze decisions and report findings to top management.

The big question is, however, whether decision analysis will become an integrated part of management's decision making. As C. Jackson Grayson has persuasively argued, the integration requires that the cultural gap between management scientists and managers be bridged. Without the bridge, personalized decision analysis, like operations research and other analytic techniques, may never be more than an optional aid, albeit interesting.

For the integration to take place, managers will have to become more skilled at using decision analysis and its practitioners more effective than they are now. In other words, analysts and managers-to-be need to undergo extensive training in the integration of decision analysis with existing organizational and personal decision processes. (This training would go far beyond the teaching of particular techniques, which is as far as most business schools go now.) The integration may also require organizational changes in control and reward structures in business.

At present, appropriate professional training is not readily available to either the manager or the specialized decision analyst. What is needed is a course of study (and supporting research) that integrates the logical, the psychological, and the organizational aspects of applied subjective decision analysis. This will probably not become available until there is at least one institute of research and teaching devoted to all aspects of decision-aiding technology (including personalized analysis) and to their integration.

This training would require overcoming the institutional rigidities associated with partitioning universities along such traditional departmental lines as engineering, psychology, business, and statistics. Even within single departments such as business, the feeder disciplines—organizational behavior, applied mathematics, finance, business policy, and marketing—are usually kept jealously apart. If these can be adequately synthesized, management science in general, and personalized decision analysis in particular, can at last achieve full-fledged assimilation into the day-to-day business of management. ▽

Reprint 82511

References

1 See C. Jackson Grayson,
Decisions Under Uncertainty
(Boston: Division of Research,
Harvard University Graduate School of
Business Administration, 1960)
and "Management Science and
Business Practice,"
HBR July-August 1973, p. 41.

2 See Rex V. Brown,
"Do Managers Find Decision Theory Useful?"
HBR May-June 1970, p.78,
and Howard Raiffa and Robert O. Schlaifer,
Applied Statistical Decision Theory
(Boston: Division of Research,
Harvard University Graduate School of
Business Administration, 1962).

3 See, for example, John F. Magee,
"Decision Trees for Decision Making,"
HBR July-August 1964, p. 126,
or the more recent article by
Samuel E. Bodily,
"When Should You Go to Court?"
HBR May-June 1981, p. 103.

4 See David B. Hertz,
"Risk Analysis in Capital Investment,"
HBR January-February1964, p. 95,
and John S. Hammond III,
"Better Decisions with Preference Theory,"
HBR November-December 1967, p. 123,
for descriptions of risk profiles
and utility functions, respectively.

5 Michael E. Porter,
Competitive Strategy
(New York: The Free Press, 1980),
pp. 299-357.

6 A comprehensive treatment of multi-
attribute utility analysis is provided by
Ralph L. Keeney and Howard Raiffa in
*Decisions with Multiple Objectives:
Preferences and Value Trade-offs*
(New York: Wiley, 1976).
Our example illustrates only the
basic ideas of the method and the sim-
plest form of analysis, linear and additive.

7 *The Art and Science of Negotiation,*
a forthcoming book by Howard Raiffa
(Cambridge: Belknap Press of
Harvard University Press)
will contain an extensive treatment
of this subject.
Jacob W. Ulvila's doctoral dissertation,
"Decisions with Multiple Objectives
in Integrative Bargaining"
(Harvard Business School, 1979),
also addresses this topic.

The Tables Turned

Up! up! my friend, and quit your books,
Or surely you'll grow double:
Up! up! my friend, and clear your looks;
Why all this toil and trouble?

The sun, above the mountain's head,
A freshening lustre mellow
Through all the long green fields has spread,
His first sweet evening yellow.

Books! 'tis a dull and endless strife:
Come, hear the woodland linnet,
How sweet his music! on my life
There's more of wisdom in it.

And hark! how blithe the throstle sings!
He, too, is no mean preacher:
Come forth into the light of things,
Let Nature be your teacher.

She has a world of ready wealth,
Our minds and hearts to bless—
Spontaneous wisdom breathed by health,
Truth breathed by cheerfulness.

One impulse from a vernal wood
May teach you more of man,
Of moral evil and of good,
Than all the sages can.

Sweet is the lore which Nature brings;
Our meddling intellect
Misshapes the beauteous forms of things:—
We murder to dissect.

Enough of science and of art!
Close up those barren leaves;
Come forth, and bring with you a heart
That watches and receives.

William Wordsworth, 1798

Keeping Informed

*Refined research methods
provide another source of information
for analyzing complex issues*

*Until recently, decision makers in
business have had to rely largely
on intuition, experience, and
luck when wrestling with
tough-to-quantify trade-offs
in multiple-choice situations. But
now, refined quantitative tools
are gaining favor among managers
in leading companies as another
source of information for analyzing
complex issues and confirming
intuitive impressions. This discussion is focused primarily for the
information user, who should
be aware of the various quantitative
methods and their usefulness.*

*Mr. Heenan is dean of the
College of Business Administration at the University of
Hawaii, where he also serves as
professor of management. Most
recently, he was vice president for
Executive Planning and Development at Citicorp and Citibank in
New York. Mr. Addleman is
president of Barr & Company, a
Philadelphia-based consulting
firm specializing in the application
of quantitative techniques to
business problems.*

*David A. Heenan and
Robert B. Addleman*

Quantitative techniques for today's decision makers

"The Executive Knocking Block," a simple piece of walnut, is one novelty company's recent offering to supersti- tious managers who, at decision-mak- ing time, find themselves surrounded by only steel and glass. Frivolous as this gimmick sounds, it underlines well the role that luck still plays in many corporate decisions. This need to rely upon luck is, at least in part, a consequence of the increasingly complex and subjective nature of con- temporary business. Many important issues seem to defy quantification, and decision makers are often forced to rely on their intuition and experience to a greater degree than may be de- sirable.

For today's managers, the dilemma is expecially worrisome. Consider the plight of the airline executive. He knows that potential air travelers wish- ing to fly coast-to-coast have many air- lines from which to choose. All have nearly identical aircraft types, rate structures, efficiency, and safety rec- ords. How does the concerned manager determine the comparative advantage of his carrier from the rest of the pack? And more important, how can this superiority be conveyed to the travel- ing public? In the airlines, as in other industries, decision makers are finding answers with a "new" generation of analytical techniques.

Labeled *multivariate analysis* (MVA), the quantitative methods can help to evaluate the complex and intangible factors that influence consumers. Though MVA is not really new, until recently its application to business problems had been confined largely to the consumer packaged goods and ser vices sector.

But now, decision makers in many other businesses are discovering MVA, for example, as a way (a) to measure more accurately consumer perceptions and preferences and (b) to reduce the risks associated with new product de- velopment. They discount the notion that a customer selects, say, a bank exclusively on the basis of tangible marketing appeals like its interest rate on savings or convenience of location. What about the intangibles, they are asking, such as the way the public perceives one bank's personality versus another's? Until recently, managers had no way to measure and rank the relative importance of these intangible consumer preferences.

Equally important are the trade-offs consumers and businessmen make in typical multichoice situations: Will a buyer of breakfast foods forgo a leading brand name for greater nutritional value? Will a new car purchaser prefer size over price, fuel economy, or trade-in value? Will the air traveler forfeit any one of several frills in favor of cheaper air fares? How will the corporate decision maker act when choosing among several investment proposals or new plant sites?

Most of the decisions we, as consumers and businessmen, make are multidimensional, and MVA's recent refinements enable us to analyze these tough-to-quantify trade-offs. It is because MVA can sort through the objective as well as subjective aspects of the consumer selection process that its applicability is especially appealing to today's manager.

This article will describe how quantitative techniques are being used to guide managers in a wide range of companies. While the focus is on external customer markets, some of the most interesting MVA applications have been on internal personnel problems and these, too, we will discuss.

A matter of choice

Decision makers exposed to multivariate analysis for the first time invariably ask, "How do I know which method to use?" Two simple rules of technique selection should be followed.

First, and most important, be aware of the data requirements of each method. As shown in *Exhibit I*, multivariate techniques can be classified on the basis of two possible uses—*prediction* or *description*[1]—and we will discuss both of these in the following sections.

Second, outline the questions to be answered before starting the analysis. This suggestion may sound trite, but it is critical. Nowadays far too much analysis is being conducted on a "needle in the haystack" basis—where the decision maker sifts through mountains of data for relevant bits of information. The outcome, more often

than not, is much wasted effort with few tangible results.

But when the key issues are well defined in advance, MVA can be invaluable. Prior identification of the questions to be answered also affects the sequence in which the various techniques should be applied. Important technical efficiencies, primarily on the programming side, are gained by applying these tools in the proper order.

To illustrate our case more fully, we will offer examples of several multivariate techniques in action. For space reasons, our discussion of these methods will be brief. However, the interested reader may find a more complete technical treatment in the footnoted references.

Prediction methods

The distinguishing feature of predictive techniques is that one or several variables are said to be a function of some other variables. For instance, the automobile industry seeks to predict annual new car sales with information from the Gross National Product, consumer price index, annual scrappage rates of old automobiles, and a host of other factors. Thus annual new car sales are dependent on, or are a function of, these variables.

Multiple regression is one popular predictive technique used by decision makers when the data are quantitative or numerical. However, prediction may also involve qualitative or state-of-being information.

For example, bankers use another multivariate technique, known as discriminant analysis, to assess whether an individual will be a good or poor credit risk based upon personal financial data. Here a qualitative variable, credit rating, is a function of a person's income, financial obligations, and so forth.

For the most part, multivariate techniques deal with both qualitative and quantitative data to estimate possible relationships. Five of the most popular prediction methods that we will

now discuss are conjoint measurement, discriminant analysis, multiple regression, automatic interaction detection, and canonical analysis.

Conjoint measurement: The subject of a recent HBR article, this technique is especially useful for evaluating consumer preferences.[2] Its underlying principle is somewhat novel but relatively simple to understand: conjoint measurement is used when the decision maker seeks to predict an ordered arrangement of information from two or more variables. This ordering is assumed to be a function of a series of qualitative predictors.

With the aid of canned computer programs, this process of prediction derives quantitative scale values from qualitative information.[3] The ordering to be estimated represents unique combinations of factors that have been arranged by surveyed consumers in a "most preferred" to "least preferred" sequence. Although each combination is unique, the individual must make trade-offs in order to complete the preference sequence.

The computer program begins by breaking down this ordering into its component parts. Simultaneously, a numerical value is assigned to each component based on its relative importance in the ranked sequence. The more times an individual "trades off" a specific component, the lower the numerical value assigned to that particular item.

The program continues to adjust the size of the values until it finds a set that when added together will match the original ordered sequence as nearly

1. This classification is based on one proposed by Thomas C. Kinnear and James K. Taylor, "Multivariate Methods in Marketing Research: A Further Attempt at Classification," *Journal of Marketing*, October 1971, p. 56.

2. See Paul E. Green and Yoram Wind, "New Way to Measure Consumers' Judgments," HBR July-August 1975, p. 107; see also Paul E. Green and Yoram Wind, *Multiattribute Decisions in Marketing: A Measurement Approach* (Hinsdale, Ill.: Dryden Press, 1973).

3. For information on conventional MVA software packages, see W.J. Dixon, ed., *Biomedical Computer Programs* (Los Angeles: School of Medicine, University of California, 1973); and Louis Nie, *Statistical Package for the Social Sciences*, 2d ed. (New York: McGraw-Hill, 1975).

Exhibit I
A classification of multivariate methods

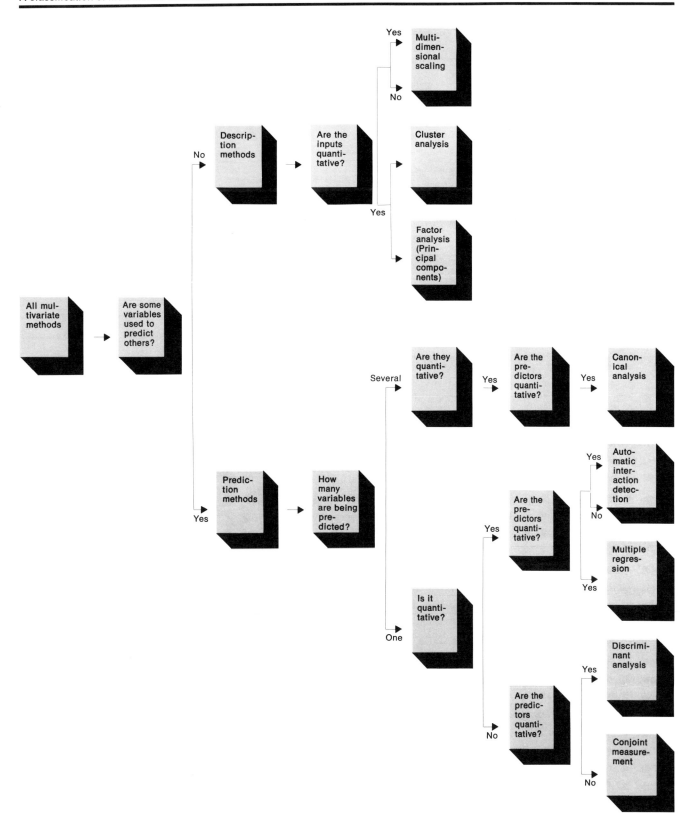

as possible. Called "utility scores," these numerical values reflect the relative importance of each component to the consumer.

By allowing the manager to measure the utility associated with many factors that could not otherwise be quantified, conjoint measurement has a wide range of applications. For example, decision makers are using this technique to accomplish such different ends as tracking the *youth market*, modifying *movie prices*, and developing cost-effective *compensation programs*.

Of particular interest to many companies is the *youth market*, representing an estimated $200 billion in annual purchasing power, besides setting the fashion pace for other consumer groups. It is no wonder that decision makers are trying to assess how young singles allocate their take-home pay.

This segment was asked by a leading bank how they would prefer to use their income. What were the trade-offs and their relative importance to youth when deciding to spend, save, or invest their discretionary income? In other words, what were the expenditure preferences of this sample of young consumers?

More specifically, the bank was interested in the relative utility to young consumers of 12 spending choices:

1. Buy a sailboat
2. Buy a new automobile
3. Buy clothes
4. Buy furniture
5. Travel overseas
6. Travel in the United States
7. Start my own business
8. Deposit money in a savings account
9. Continue my education
10. Get married
11. Invest in the stock market
12. Invest in a home

From this list, various combinations of these 12 options were constructed. An experimental design was used to determine which options should be included in each set and to reduce to

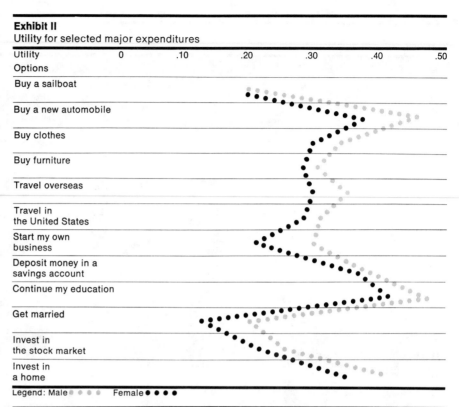

Exhibit II
Utility for selected major expenditures

Legend: Male ○ ○ ○ ○ Female ● ● ● ●

a manageable number the sets to be ordered by consumers.[4] This ordering provided the input to the conjoint measurement program.

By asking singles to rank the combinations in order of "most preferred" to "least preferred," managers determined utility scores for these options. As indicated in *Exhibit II*, these young consumers possess the highest utility for buying a new automobile, continuing their education, and investing in a home, plus a moderately high utility for depositing money in a savings account. Based on this information, the bank developed a new service for its youth market known as the "Young Professional's Account."

Coupled with simulation analysis, which projects changes by varying certain controllable factors, conjoint measurement is helping other companies to assess difficult pricing decisions during periods of economic uncertainty.[5] Probably nowhere does this uncertainty reign more than in the motion picture industry. Even with strong demand for cinema entertainment, distributors still want to know what strategy of *movie prices* will

maximize their box office receipts over the long run.

Recently a motion picture distributor sought to determine how much utility was associated with the alternatives for each of the following three factors:

Admission price: $1.00, $2.00, or $3.00.
Theater location: city center, suburb, or shopping mall.
Feature time: afternoon, early evening, or late evening.

Conjoint measurement indicated that movie-goers were highly sensitive to price regardless of the time of day or theater location. With simulation analysis, it was also possible to estimate how much attendance could be increased by decreasing the price of admission. Since this analysis, a number of theaters have adopted a "dollar-at-all-times" policy, resulting in a significant resurgence in attendance. In

4. B.J. Winer, *Statistical Principles in Experimental Design*, 2d ed. (New York: McGraw-Hill, 1971).

5. A very useful introduction to simulation procedures is found in Claude McMillan and Richard R. Gonzales, *Systems Analysis: A Computer Approach to Decision Models*, rev. ed. (Homewood, Ill.: Richard D. Irwin, 1968).

this and many other cases, conjoint techniques coupled with simulation analysis are helping managers experiment with "what-if" thinking by anticipating the possible business consequences of their proposed actions.

So far we have focused on multivariate approaches to analyzing the external consumer market for various goods and services. Yet some of the most effective applications of MVA have been directed to the "internal market," the company's work force. By evaluating their staff members with the same degree of sophistication that they examine their product markets, some companies are beginning to experience significant payoffs. Consider some recent cases of effective internal use.

Over the years, a plethora of complex and costly executive *compensation programs* has been developed by major corporations and their consultants. But, frequently, the variety of these compensation alternatives camouflages the fundamental question: What do top executives really want in a pay package?

Virtually ignored are the trade-offs that an executive will make among alternative forms of compensation.[6] Only when he or she is confronted with the thought of forfeiting less important forms of compensation for more essential ones is it possible to measure the relative importance of each fringe benefit.

Using conjoint measurement, we examined the benefit preferences of executives in one major multinational corporation. From *Exhibit III*, note that their greatest preference was for four weeks annual vacation, with health insurance and low interest loans also ranking quite high.

In our follow-up interviews, sampled executives frequently commented about the pressures of executive life and the need to "get away from it all," or, at the very least, the need to cover the risks to their health with insurance. To some extent, this feedback suggests the growing concern of today's executives for maintaining the quality of their own lives.

Significantly, little interest was expressed in financial advisory and planning services or split-dollar life insurance—two programs that the company evaluated as critically important to its managers. Armed with this new information about executive pay preferences, the senior vice president for personnel relations was able to structure the management compensation program at a considerable cost saving.

A one-bank holding company used this same type of analysis, based on the following questions, to help determine the similarities and differences of managers in its traditional banking and congeneric businesses:

What forms of variable compensation, if any, are needed to motivate its venture capitalists versus commercial bankers? Should a premium be given to MBAs entering the firm's consulting subsidiary over those joining the rest of the institution? How important are bank titles to managers in the consumer finance company?

By ranking those features that managers perceive to be most important, conjoint measurement helped to answer some of these questions.

For other companies, similar issues are being resolved. One midwestern chemical company, faced with widespread pressure to reduce expenses, is examining the trade-off of pay cuts rather than layoffs for its sales and research staffs. Related concern exists over the form and magnitude of the proposed pay cuts, the length of possible layoffs, and the acceptability to the staff of all possible options.

To date, MVA has enabled senior management to see the range of these alternatives and to prepare a more rational plan of action than might ordinarily have occurred.

Discriminant analysis: Often, there are minute differences in consumer preferences that cannot be determined by simply "eyeballing" the data. And frequently, trends that are discernible in the statistics appear to be the direct results of certain actions; in fact, they may be due to nothing more

6. Wilbur G. Lewellen and Howard P. Lanser, "Executive Pay Preferences," HBR September-October 1973, p. 115.

Exhibit III
Utility functions for alternative fringe benefits

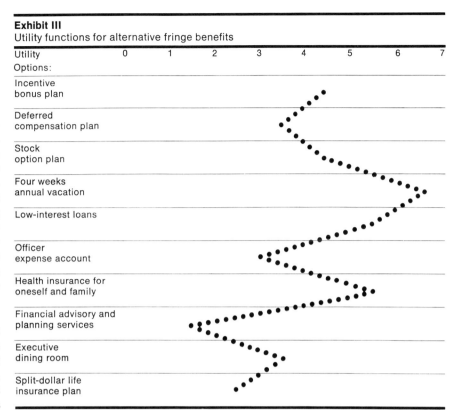

than coincidental variations in the data. *Exhibit II* suggests that males have a greater utility for many of the spending options than do females. But are these differences statistically significant? Managers are using another MVA tool, known as discriminant analysis, to answer such questions.[7]

This predictive technique tries to define a functional relationship for assigning individuals or stimuli to various groups. In other words, it attempts to classify an observation into one of several a priori groupings dependent upon the observation's individual characteristics.[8]

By maximizing the ratio of intergroup to intragroup differences, discriminant analysis pinpoints those factors that account for the largest amount of difference between groups. Moreover, its primary use is to make predictions in problems where qualitative information (e.g., good versus bad credit risks) is determined by quantitative data.

In our earlier example of expenditure preferences, bank managers applied discriminant analysis to the utility scores of young singles to determine which specific spending options are statistically greater for males than for females. This situation is the case in only two instances—the decisions to "buy an automobile" and to "start my own business." Accordingly, heavily male-oriented advertising themes were

designed by the bank for its new car and small business loans.

Ironically, discriminant analysis is also being actively used to evaluate the statistical validity of "discrimination" complaints. For anyone concerned with affirmative action planning, the question of interpreting statistics is critical. Are the company's employment, salary, and promotional practices discriminatory in a statistically significant sense?

Some companies are finding this technique to be effective in monitoring the vital concept of "parity" in their organization. EEO officers are now able to reduce the costly and time-consuming threat of litigation by prescreening affirmative action complaints for statistical validity.

Especially for those companies in the enviable position of having a computerized data base of their work force, it is possible to monitor the relative progress of various groups over time. The salary progression of, say, women versus men employed internationally in the company's sales force can be measured; cross-functional opportunities for Spanish-speaking Americans can be compared with other EEO classes; and so on.

Now decision makers are using additional applications of discriminant analysis on problems ranging from the prediction of corporate bankruptcies to the likelihood of successful joint ventures.[9]

Multiple regression: This familiar workhorse of analytical techniques has been around for many years. But, with the availability of recent computer packages, its level of sophistication has been upgraded considerably.

It borrows from the fundamental feature of regression analysis: the mathematical fitting of a smooth trend line (or trend surface, if more than two variables are involved) to the relationship between variables.[10]

Hence, the idea behind regression is that all observations of a variable are best explained by this fitted line, which is simply the calculated best fit

of a trend line to the relationship between two sets of measurements—measurements such as the relationship between the age and income level of a group of potential customers.

Since most of the phenomena in which managers are interested are the result of the action of more than a single factor, the uses of multiple regression are many and varied. Most often it is used to measure how much the value of a particular quantitative factor can be identified from the knowledge of several forces working together.

For instance, the interested decision maker might wish to see how closely the sales of a particular product can be predicted from some kind of measurement of the quality and the amount of advertising, the sales promotion effort, the distribution network, and the income prospects of potential buyers. If such historical data are available, the relationships between these variables can be measured.

For bank executives analyzing the youth market in our earlier example, multiple regression was used to predict the chances of success of the Young Professional's Account for savings. By examining an earlier and somewhat similar product for youths, "Hassle-Free Checking," it was possible to isolate several important characteristics of young singles that influenced sales of this service. Mindful of these special traits, marketers incorporated the appropriate appeals into their new savings account campaign.

Automatic interaction detection: Of special interest to the bank's decision makers was whether some people have a greater-than-average propensity to save than others, and if so, what their personal characteristics are. Using the individual utility scores derived from conjoint measurement, it was possible to answer these questions with automatic interaction detection (AID).[11]

AID seeks to explain key variations in a quantitative factor by performing a succession of two-way splits upon a series of qualitative and quantitative predictors. In our example, the utility

7. See Paul E. Green and Donald S. Tull, *Research for Marketing Decisions*, 3d ed. (Englewood Cliffs, N.J.: Prentice Hall, 1975), or Donald G. Morrison, "On the Interpretation of Discriminant Analysis," *Journal of Marketing Research*, May 1969, p. 156.

8. Edward I. Altman, "Financial Ratios, Discriminant Analysis and the Prediction of Corporate Bankruptcy," *Journal of Finance*, September 1968, p. 591.

9. Ibid., p. 589.

10. For a general discussion, see Chester R. Wasson, *Understanding Quantitative Analysis* (New York: Appleton-Century Crofts, 1969), p. 210; for greater depth, see N.R. Draper and H. Smith, *Applied Regression Analysis* (New York: John Wiley, 1966).

11. A thorough discussion of AID can be found in J.A. Sonquist, E.L. Baker, and J.N. Morgan, *Searching for Structure (Alias AID-III)* (Survey Research Center, University of Michigan, 1971), and related techniques in F. Andrews, J. Morgan, and J. Sonquist, *Multiple Classification Analysis* (Survey Research Center, University of Michigan, 1967); also see Richard Staelin, "Another Look at AID," *Journal of Advertising Research*, October 1971, p. 23.

Exhibit IV
AID summary tree (larger mean values represent greater likelihood to save)

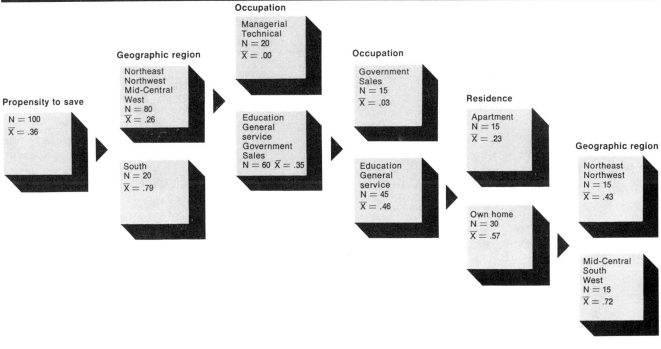

to deposit money in a savings account (really, the propensity to save) is a function of a person's sex, age, income, occupation, and so on. The AID summary tree in *Exhibit IV* illustrates how this predictive technique helped to isolate blocs of individuals with the highest utility to save.

As shown in this exhibit, from an average propensity to save of .36 for the entire sample, the program split the sample into subgroups whose scores differed most from that of the overall average.

Hence approximately one fifth of the sample possessed a propensity to save of .70 or higher. These rather intense savers tended to reside in the mid-central, southern, and western regions of the United States.

Conversely, those least likely to save were identified by their occupation, with managerial and technical job-holders leading the pack.

Canonical analysis: As with the previous findings, the bank's executives pressed on for even more valuable in-

formation. Next, they asked, what predictive relationships exist between individuals' utility scores (derived from conjoint measurement) and their personal characteristics? And which of these relationships are statistically meaningful?

While AID can identify potential relationships, it's use is questionable on the matter of statistical significance. For answers to both questions, canonical analysis is the appropriate tool. This method tries to identify which sets of variables are most closely associated with each other and thus account for the greatest reduction of variability in the data.[12] Generally, more than one pair of correlated items are identified, with each successive pair accounting for the largest amount of the remaining difference.

What canonical analysis revealed in our bank example is that the savings habits of young consumers are most highly correlated with geography—and this relationship is significant indeed. Other meaningful relationships, such as the entrepreneurial spirit and masculinity, are also reconfirmed.

Still, predictive information of this variety is not enough. Like so many other attempts to estimate precise associations, these methods meet the twin frustrations of inadequate data quality and unstable, discontinuous relationships. Consequently, decision makers are turning to a new generation of quantitative techniques.

Description techniques

For those managers not concerned with prediction, descriptive multivariate tools may provide added meaning to a data base. What at first glance may appear to be a sterile and uninteresting set of facts regarding, say, consumer attitudes toward a new product design can often be transformed into most valuable information with the aid of these techniques.

Three of the most popular that we will discuss are factor analysis, cluster analysis, and multidimensional scaling. While most descriptive methods re-

12. Green and Tull, *Research For Marketing Decisions.*

quire quantitative inputs, some versions also accept qualitative data.

Factor analysis: Psychographic segmentation—that is, identifying marketing segments on the basis of life-style or personality traits—is becoming a favorite method of evaluating new market opportunities.[13] While neither life-style nor personality represents observable variables, positive inferences can still be drawn from consumer attitudes and preferences. Here factor analysis helps by summarizing a large number of variables into a smaller, more concise body of information.

Unlike predictive aids, factor analysis looks for descriptive relationships in the data. One popular version, *principal components analysis*, finds a series of new variables which, while mutually independent, accounts for the most difference in the original data.[14]

In seeking to explain as much variability as possible, this method makes a series of passes through the original data. Each pass produces a component that is uncorrelated with the previous ones and accounts for the largest amount of variation remaining in the data. The first variable, or principal component, derived from this analysis often is a useful index of behavior for psychographic segmentation.

Besides assessing the spending profiles of potential consumers, the bank used principal components analysis to survey young singles about their leisure time preferences. In all, 40 utility scores were obtained for each subject. Typically, however, a person has a high utility for some items but a low utility for others.

13. Ronald E. Frank, William F. Massey, and Yoram Wind, *Market Segmentation* (Englewood Cliffs, N.J.: Prentice Hall, 1972), Chapter 2.

14. See John E. Overall and C. James Klett, *Applied Multivariate Analysis* (New York: McGraw-Hill, 1972).

15. Further details on cluster analysis can be found in David A. Aaker, ed., *Multivariate Analysis in Marketing: Theory and Application* (Belmont, Cal.: Wadsworth Publishing Co., 1971).

16. See Paul E. Green and Vithala R. Rao, *Applied Multidimensional Scaling* (New York: Holt, Rinehart, and Winston, 1972), and Paul E. Green and Frank J. Carmone, *Multidimensional Scaling and Related Techniques in Marketing Analysis* (Boston, Mass.: Allyn and Bacon, 1970).

Exhibit V

Life-style index scores derived from principal components analysis

Subject 1	2.0
Subject 2	−0.1
Subject 3	0.2
Subject 4	2.5
Subject 5	1.8
Subject 6	1.4
Subject 7	−0.1
Subject 8	−0.9
Subject 9	−1.9
Subject 10	−1.8

That, of course, makes it almost impossible to draw meaningful inferences about potential consumers. But, with the help of principal components analysis, it is possible to consolidate such information into a single scale value—in this case, a life-style index.

Exhibit V shows the life-style scores, derived from principal components analysis, for just 10 young singles. A high score on this index suggests an active or swinging life-style; a low score, a sedate or domesticated style.

Although interesting, the findings obtained from principal components analysis were still too imprecise. In its one-dimensional, index form, it obscured more meaningful information regarding the particular life-style characteristics of both swingers and nonswingers. For help, the bank turned to another multivariate technique.

Cluster analysis: The life-style scores derived from principal components analysis were submitted to cluster analysis. The logic behind all clustering programs is the same: to segregate variables into those subgroups with the greatest similarity.[15]

Thus, unlike discriminant analysis, where stimuli are assigned to various categories based upon a set of predictors, cluster analysis forms groups of stimuli based upon their commonality.

This is accomplished with a computer program that minimizes variability within groups, while maximizing differences between groups.

Applied to our example, cluster analysis revealed two dominant life-styles among singles. One subgroup consisted of singles with moderately high scores on the life-style index, while a second subgroup consisted of singles with relatively low scores on the index. Very different features characterized each group. Comparing swingers with nonswingers, the bank found the following difference in personal characteristics:

Swingers
High school graduates
Blue-collar occupations
In their early-to-mid 20s
Located in Northeast and Northwest
Apartment dwellers

Nonswingers
Attended graduate school
White-collar occupations
In their late 20s to mid-30s
Located in Mid-Central, South,
    and West
Homeowners

With this information, marketing officers were able to segment the youth market into more definitive clusters. For them, high priority segments were potential automobile and housing borrowers. Based on these findings, innovative car and condominium loans have been developed.

Multidimensional scaling: To assess their corporate image compared with the competition's, today's decision makers rely on still another form of MVA called multidimensional scaling, which can help them sort out those companies or products that compete most effectively with each other and on what terms they do this.[16]

Simply stated, this technique attempts to map consumers' perceptions of similarity as distances in a perceptual space.

The input to multidimensional scaling consists of consumer judgments chart-

Exhibit VI
Multidimensional mapping/
two-dimensional configuration

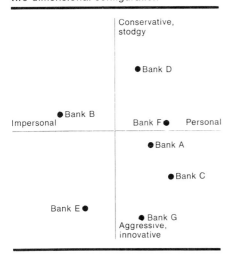

ed on a multipoint rating scale of similarity and difference.

For example, a pair of stimuli that are perceived as almost identical might be assigned a numerical value of "2" by the consumer; another pair perceived as quite different might be assigned a value of "9." With this data, scaling programs map the relative position of stimuli on the basis of association.

By positioning these stimuli in a geometric space, this method identifies the major dimensions (axes) of comparison used by consumers. Although multidimensional scaling programs do not interpret the dimensions, a skilled analyst can usually infer possible interpretations from other information obtained from respondents.

Exhibit VI shows how the public in a major eastern market views the banking industry. On the basis of two dimensions, shown as axes, customers in this survey tended to distinguish banks on their personalism and their ability to change. The findings have raised some executive eyebrows.

As shown in this exhibit, client Bank A, which views itself as a pacesetter with a warmly human touch, was surprised to see that it is categorized as

17. Our approach is an alternative to the conventional one presented in Herbert E. Meyer, "A Computer May Be Deciding What You Get Paid," *Fortune*, November 1973, p. 168.

relatively stodgy and somewhat heavy-handed. Executives in Bank A were even more shocked to learn that the public perceives their bank as most similar to Bank C and Bank F—two institutions that are troubled with deteriorating market shares and pressure from local consumer groups.

Fortunately for Bank A, its senior managers were able to recover from the shock of what they saw as a most undesirable profile. In short order, the bank launched aggressive advertising and public relations programs designed to enhance its external image. Without the technological advantages of multidimensional scaling, this gap between the attitudes of management and those of its potential customer base might have gone undetected.

Another interesting application involved the use of multidimensional scaling to establish a new system of salary administration. Senior officers in one high growth manufacturing company became disenchanted with the system of salary administration that had been in place for many years. For help they turned to computer-assisted multivariate techniques.[17]

To develop appropriate criteria for a new salary schedule, the officers were asked to compare the 15 top executive positions in the company on whatever basis they felt was relevant. By analyzing their responses with multidimensional scaling, it was possible to determine the perceived lines of authority in the company as well as the relative importance of executive positions on several key dimensions.

This analysis led to an improved salary system devoid of many of the earlier inequities. Perhaps even more important was management's new sense in "customizing" this program to meet its own particular needs.

Caution note

Former Treasury Secretary George M. Humphrey was once quoted as saying, "There are no hard decisions, just insufficient facts. When you have the facts, the decisions come easy." Man-

agers today can take little comfort in Humphrey's remarks. More often than not, they are bombarded with facts—even to the point where effective decision making is retarded, not promoted.

By consolidating a multitude of data, MVA methods can help the modern-day manager. And the examples given in this article represent just some of the latest quantitative methods that are being used by leading companies to understand their businesses more fully.

The barnstorming aviator who used to fly by the seat of his pants has been replaced by pilots using sophisticated instruments. Still, even with elaborate navigational aids, pilots do not take off in a heavy ground fog.

Similarly, multivariate techniques do not replace the decision maker. Instead, they provide another source of information for analyzing complex issues or confirming "gut-feel" impressions.

And, like any decision tool, MVA has its limitations. Analyses, predictive or descriptive, conducted with these qualitative methods can only be as good as the data input. Moreover, specific techniques have specific limitations.

Hence it is debatable how well a ranking of hypothetical factors in conjoint measurement portrays actual decision making. Clearly, it can never encompass all the variables that motivate human behavior. Automatic interaction detection is best suited for large samples of at least a thousand or more observations; discarding all but the first principal component in principal components analysis can mean sacrificing a considerable amount of information; and so on.

It is also easy to become captivated by canned multivariate programs and to forget that the numbers generated must make business sense. Still, by gaining an awareness of these techniques and their shortcomings, decision makers can avoid the pitfall of quantitative alchemy, that modern-day plague.

Nonquantitative
Decision Making

*Good managers, like doctors, know how
to make decisions based on sketchy information.*

Humble Decision Making

by Amitai Etzioni

Decision making in the 1990s will be even more of an art and less of a science than it is today. Not only is the world growing more complex and uncertain at a faster and faster pace, but the old decision-making models are failing, and we can expect their failure to accelerate as well.

If executives once imagined they could gather enough information to read the business environment like an open book, they have had to dim their hopes. The flow of information has swollen to such a flood that managers are in danger of drowning; extracting relevant data from the torrent is increasingly a daunting task. Little wonder that some beleaguered decision makers – even outside the White House – turn to astrologers and mediums.

Yet from this swelling confusion, a new decision-making model is evolving, one more attuned to a world that resembles not so much an open book as an entire library of encyclopedias under perpetual revision. This new approach – in fact a very old approach in modern dress – understands that executives must often proceed with only partial information, which, moreover, they have had no time to fully process or analyze. I call this model "humble decision making."

Amitai Etzioni, university professor at George Washington University, wrote this article while serving as visiting professor at the Harvard Business School. His most recent book is The Moral Dimension: Toward a New Economics *(Free Press, 1988).*

In a simpler age, the principle governing business decisions was held to be rationalism. Rationalists argued that decision makers should and *could* explore every route that might lead to their goal, collect information about the costs and utility of each, systematically compare these various alternatives, and choose the most effective course. Executives were then urged to throw the full power of their leadership behind the chosen path. The rule was: Implement!

How do you make a decision when there's too much data and too little time?

Overcome every adversity! This called for the kind of assertiveness shown by Israeli army commanders when they order subordinates to storm and take a roadblock: "I don't care if you go over it, under it, around it, or through it, just see that it's ours by the end of the day."

Today's typical executive finds it quite impossible to pursue decisions this aggressively. For example, it is no longer enough to understand the U.S. economy; events in Brazil, Kuwait, Korea, and a score of other countries are likely to affect one's decisions. Explosive innovation in fields like communications, biotechnology, and superconductivity can take companies by surprise. Unexpected developments can affect the cost of everything from raw materials to health care—witness the oil shocks of the 1970s and the spread of AIDS in the 1980s. Economic forecasts are proving to be much less reliable than they used to be (or, perhaps, than we used to think they were). Deregulation, computer-driven program trading, foreign hot money in the U.S. economy—all add unpredictability.

Rationalist decision makers simply need to *know* much more than ever before. Of course, with computers our capacity to collect and to semiprocess information has grown, but information is not the same as knowledge. The production of knowledge is analogous to the manufacture of any other product. We begin with the raw material of facts (of which we often have a more than adequate supply). We pretreat these by means of classification, tabulation, summary, and so on, and then proceed to the assembly of correlations and comparisons. But the final product, conclusions, does not simply roll off the production line. Indeed, without powerful overarching explanatory schemes (or theories), whatever knowledge there is in the mountain of data we daily amass is often invisible.

And our prevailing theories—in economics, for instance—are proving ever less suitable to the new age. Artificial intelligence may someday make the mass production of knowledge an easy matter, but certainly not before the year 2000.

In short, the executives of today and tomorrow face continuing information overloads but little growth in the amount of knowledge usable for most complex managerial decisions. Decision makers in the 1990s will continue to travel on unmarked, unlit roads in rain and fog rather than on the broad, familiar, sunlit streets of their own hometowns.

Actually, decision making was never quite as easy as rationalists would have us think. Psychologists argue compellingly that even before our present troubles began, human minds could not handle the complexities that important decisions entailed. Our brains are too limited. At best, we can focus on eight facts at a time. Our ability to calculate probabilities, especially to combine two or more probabilities—essential for most decision making—is low. And the evidence shows that we learn surprisingly slowly. We make the same mistakes over and over again, adjusting our estimates and expectations at an agonizing crawl, and quite poorly at that.

Moreover, we are all prone to let our emotions get in the way—fear, for one. Since all decisions entail risks, decision making almost inevitably evokes anxiety. Decision makers respond in predictable ways that render their decisions less reasonable. Irving L.

Janis and Leon Mann have treated this subject at some length in their book, *Decision Making.* Common patterns include defensive avoidance (delaying decisions unduly), overreaction (making decisions impulsively in order to escape the anxious state), and hypervigilance (obsessively collecting more and more information instead of making a decision).

Political factors are another complicating consideration, partly because we try to deny their importance. One study reports that most executives see their decisions as professional, even technocratic, but rarely as political. While they acknowledge that political considerations may enter into dealings with a labor union or a local government and that "bad" political corporations do exist, few are willing to recognize that all corporations are political entities and, consequently, that most if not all important decisions have a political dimension. For example, it is not enough to dream up a new product, market, or

Half the choices you make every day are, in theory, impossibly complex.

research project; we must consider how to build up bases of support among vice presidents, division leaders, and others.

By disregarding the emotions and politics of decision making, rationalism has taught executives to expect more of themselves than is either possible or, indeed, desirable. Implicit in the rationalistic decision model is the assumption that decision makers have unqualified power and wisdom. It ignores the fact that other individuals, too, set goals for themselves and seek to push them through. For ethical reasons, we should not want to override them, and for practical reasons, we cannot do so. Successful decision-making strategies must necessarily include a place for cooperation, coalition building, and the whole panorama of differing personalities, perspectives, responsibilities, and powers.

So even before the world turned ultracomplex and superfungible, our intellectual limitations were such that wholly rational decisions were often beyond our grasp. Recognition of this fact led students of decision making to come up with two new approaches that are, in effect, counsels of despair.

The first of these is called incrementalism, a formal title for what is otherwise known as the science of muddling through. Incrementalism advocates moving not so much toward a goal as away from trouble, trying this or that small maneuver without any grand plan or sense of ultimate purpose. It has two attractive strengths. First, it eliminates the need for complete, encyclopedic information by focusing on limited areas, those nearest to hand, one at a time. And, second, it avoids the danger of grand policy decisions by not making any. Its main weakness is that it is highly "conservative"; it invariably chooses a direction close to the prevailing one. Grand new departures, radical changes in course, do not occur, however much they may be needed.

The second counsel of despair is openly opposed to reflection and analysis. It calls on executives to steam full speed ahead and remake the world rather than seek to understand it. Building on the perfectly accurate observation that many things are exceedingly difficult to predict—which product will sell, what the result of an ad campaign will be, how long R&D will take—executives are advised not to sit back and await sufficient information but to pick the course favored by their experience, inner voice, intuition, and whatever information is readily available—and then to commit. Pumping enough resources, dedication, and ingenuity into the course they have fixed on can make it work, can render an underprocessed decision right.

While more heroic and appealing to the executive self-image than incrementalism, this go-for-it approach is the decision maker's equivalent of "Damn the torpedoes, full speed ahead!" It is a hidden rather than an open counsel of despair, but it does despair of knowing the world and approaching it sensibly. And it is much more likely to end in shipwreck than in victory, especially in ever more treacherous seas.

Yet another approach—rarely described but not as uncommon as it ought to be—is what we might call rational ritualism, where executives and their staffs take part in an information dance whose prescribed moves include the data *pas de deux* and the interpretation waltz, except that the information used is generally poor (arbitrarily selected or from undependable sources) and often vastly overinterpreted. Usually most of those involved (or all of them) know the data is unreliable and the analysis unreal but dare not say that the emperor is naked. Instead, they make ritualistic projections—and know enough to ignore them.

A less explicitly recognized approach to decision making has been with us for centuries. Effective managers have made use of it since business began. Because this approach is particularly well suited to the new age of data overload and pell-mell change, it deserves a new look and, though still evolving, the respectability that a clear formulation can give it. I call it humble decision making, but a more descriptive title might be adaptive decision making or mixed scanning, since it entails a mixture of shallow and deep examination of data—generalized con-

sideration of a broad range of facts and choices followed by detailed examination of a focused *subset* of facts and choices.

Mixed scanning contrasts strongly with two prevailing models of decision making—rationalism and incrementalism. We have already seen that the rationalist model, which requires full scanning of all relevant data and choices, is often impossible to heed. It requires the collection of enormous quantities of facts, the use of analytic capabilities we do not command, and a knowledge of consequences that are far away in time. Many of those who despair of its usefulness tend to favor incrementalism, or muddling through.

"Damn the torpedos! Full speed ahead!" is a good way to sink a business.

But incrementalism, too, contains a self-defeating feature. Theoretically, incremental decisions are either tentative or remedial—small steps taken in the "right" direction whenever the present course proves to be wrong. But the moment decision makers evaluate their small steps—which they must do in order to determine whether or not the present course is right—they must refer to broader guidelines. These wider criteria are not formulated incrementally but have all the hallmarks of grand, *a priori* decisions, which incrementalism seeks to avoid. Yet without such guidelines, incrementalism amounts to drifting, to action without direction.

Mixed scanning, as the term suggests, involves two sets of judgments: the first are broad, fundamental choices about the organization's basic policy and direction; the second are incremental decisions that prepare the way for new, basic judgments and that implement and particularize them once they have been made. Thus mixed scanning is much less detailed and demanding than rationalistic decision making, but still broader and more comprehensive than incrementalism—and less likely to be limited to familiar alternatives.

Rationalism is a deeply optimistic approach that assumes we can learn all we need to know; mixed scanning is an adaptive strategy that acknowledges our inability to know more than part of what we would need to make a genuinely rational decision. Incrementalism is profoundly cautious and avoids decisions based on partial knowledge; mixed scanning seeks to make the best possible use of partial knowledge rather than proceed blindly with no knowledge at all.

The oldest formal use of mixed scanning is medical. It is the way doctors make decisions. Unlike incrementalists, physicians know what they want to achieve and which parts of the organism to focus on. Unlike rationalists, they do not commit all their resources on the basis of a preliminary diagnosis, and they do not wait for every conceivable scrap of personal history and scientific data before initiating treatment. Doctors survey the general health of a patient, then zero in on his or her particular complaint. They initiate a tentative treatment, and, if it fails, they try something else.

In fact, this is roughly the way effective managers, too, often make decisions. Business data are rarely unequivocal. Driving in fog and rain has always called for caution as well as a clear sense of destination, and the rules for humble yet effective decision making are much the same for doctors and executives.

Focused trial and error is probably the most widely used procedure for adapting to partial knowledge. It has two parts: knowing where to start the search for an effective intervention, and checking outcomes at intervals to adjust and modify the intervention. This approach differs significantly from what we might call outright trial and error, which assumes no knowledge at all, and from fine-tuning searches, which can occur only when knowledge is high and uncertainty low.

Focused trial and error assumes that there is important information that the executive does not have and must proceed without. It is not a question of understanding the world "correctly," of choosing a logical procedure on the basis of facts, but of feeling one's way to an effective course of action despite the lack of essential chunks of data. It is an adaptive, not a rationalistic, strategy.

Tentativeness—a commitment to revise one's course as necessary—is an essential adaptive rule. Physicians tell their patients to take a medicine for x number of days, to call them at once if the symptoms grow worse rather than better, to return after some set interval for another examination. Such safeguards permit the doctor to adjust the intervention if it proves to be ineffective or counterproductive. A good doctor does not invest prestige and ego in the treatment prescribed. On the contrary, what distinguishes

"Mr. Jones, we'd like to talk again about that loan application of yours."

good physicians from poor ones is precisely their sensitivity to changing conditions, their pronounced willingness to change directions on the basis of results, their humility in the face of reality.

Executives often render decisions on matters less well understood than many medical conditions. Hence executives, even more than physicians, are best off when they refuse to commit to an initial diagnosis and so refuse to risk dignity and stature on what is inevitably an uncertain course. By viewing each intervention as tentative or experimental, they declare that they fully expect to revise it.

A year ago, some American bankers may have thought it sounded grand to announce that they would play an important role in the new, post-1992 Europe. Now that the great difficulties of such a course have become more evident, those bankers who announced only that they would try to find a way to work within the European Community seem wiser and more prudent.

Procrastination is another adaptive rule that follows from an understanding of the limits of executive knowledge. Delay permits the collection of fresh evidence, the processing of additional data, the presentation of new options. (It can also give the problem a chance to recede untreated.) Rarely is missing the next board meeting as detrimental as it seems. If one can make a significantly strong case at a later board meeting or rezoning hearing or town meeting, the result will justify the delay.

Decision staggering is one common form of delay. If the Federal Reserve believed the discount rate should rise by 3%, it would still not make the adjustment all at once. By adjusting the rate half a point at a time, the Federal Reserve can see a partial result of its intervention under conditions similar to those in which the rest of the intervention, if necessary, will take place.

Fractionalizing is a second corollary to procrastination. Instead of spreading a single intervention over time, it treats important judgments as a series of subdecisions and may or may not also stagger them

> ## In decision making, humility is another word for staying loose.

in time. For example, a company concerned about future interest rates might raise half its needed equity now by issuing a bond and the other half later by selling an asset. Both staggering and fractionalizing allow the company to relate turning points in the decision process to turning points in the supply of information.

Hedging bets is another good adaptive rule. For instance, the less investors know about a specific company, the wiser it is to spread their investments among several stocks. The less certain they are of the stock market in general, the wiser they are to spread their investments among different instruments and areas—bonds and real estate, for example. Hedging bets will never produce a bonanza to compare with the lucky all-or-nothing, eggs-in-one-basket coup, but it is much more likely to improve long term yield and security.

Maintaining strategic reserves is another form of hedging bets. The stock market investor with a cash reserve after the crashes of 1929 or 1987 was in an excellent position to capitalize on those disasters. In a predictable, rational world, no company would need idle resources. In fact, large reserves can be a dangerous invitation to an LBO. But in a world where we have learned to expect the unexpected, we need reserves to cover unanticipated costs and to respond to unforeseen opportunities.

Reversible decisions, finally, are a way of avoiding overcommitment when only partial information is available. The simplest response to the energy crisis of the early 1970s, for example, was to turn down the thermostat during the winter and raise it during the summer. It had the additional virtue of being fully reversible in seconds. Conservation measures were more difficult to take back, but were often only moderately expensive, and a subsequent lowering of energy prices did not render them counterproductive, even if it did reduce the return on invested capital. Changing an energy source, on the other hand, was often a complex and expensive reaction to the crisis and costly to reverse. Yet a number of companies did convert from oil to coal in the 1970s and now wish they could recall a decision made on the basis of inadequate information and executive overconfidence.

This list of adaptive techniques illustrates several essential qualities of effective decision making that the textbook models miss: flexibility, caution, and the capacity to proceed with partial knowledge, to name just three. Only fools make rigid decisions and decisions with no sense of overarching purpose, while the most able executives already practice more humble decision making than I could possibly preach. They will, I predict, apply the good sense and versatility of this tested, realistic model ever more widely as the world grows more and more difficult to manage.

Reprint 89406

Decision making: going forward in reverse

Hillel J. Einhorn and Robin M. Hogarth

Busy managers analyze many situations and make hundreds of decisions every day. Why, for example, are sales up in one city but down in another? Would an investment in new equipment mean higher productivity or greater confusion? Is now a good time to look for a joint venture partner, or is it better to wait? Rarely, however, do we stop to think about how we think. Each decision is the outcome of a complex process that usually involves two different kinds of thinking: looking backward to understand the past and looking forward to predict the future.

Thinking backward is largely intuitive and suggestive; it tends to be diagnostic and requires judgment. It involves looking for patterns, making links between seemingly unconnected events, testing possible chains of causation to explain an event, and finding a metaphor or a theory to help in looking forward.

Thinking forward is different. Instead of intuition, it depends on a kind of mathematical formulation: the decision maker must assemble and weigh a number of variables and then make a prediction. Using a strategy or a rule, assessing the accuracy of each factor, and combining all the pieces of information, the decision maker arrives at a single, integrated forecast.

Although managers use both types of thinking all the time, they are often unaware of the differences. Moreover, this lack of awareness makes decision makers stumble into mental traps that yield bad decisions. By understanding thinking backward and forward, we can recognize these traps and improve our decisions.

Thinking backward

To understand how thinking backward works, think back to the days of the cave dwellers and consider the following exercise in assessing cause and effect. Imagine that you belong to a tribe that is sophisticated in methodology but primitive in science. Your tribe has very little knowledge of biology, physics, or chemistry but a very big problem – an alarming decrease in the birthrate. The problem is so severe that the tribe's statistician estimates that unless you can reverse the trend soon, the tribe will become extinct.

To respond to the crisis, the chief urgently launches a project to determine the cause of birth. As a member of the project team assigned the task of linking cause and effect, you have been assured that you will be allowed any and all forms of experimentation, including the use of your fellow tribespersons, to resolve this critical issue.

> *"Why a simple decision isn't."*

The first question, of course, is what to consider a relevant causal factor. In searching for a link between cause and effect, most people usually look first to some unusual or remarkable event or condition that preceded the effect. In this case, you might ask yourself if something unusual happened before the decline in births. You might look for evidence of the cause of the problem that is similar in some way to the outcome – similar in some physical or metaphorical way. Then you could assess the likelihood that the evidence explains the problem.

You might notice that the children in your tribe are similar in appearance to men and women who live together. This similarity could lead you to a leap of intuition backward: sexual intercourse causes pregnancy. You and the members of your study team

Hillel J. Einhorn is the Wallace W. Booth Professor of Behavioral Science at the University of Chicago Graduate School of Business and the founder and former director of its Center for Decision Research. Robin M. Hogarth is professor of behavioral science at the University of Chicago Graduate School of Business and director of the Center for Decision Research.

would probably acknowledge, however, that this theory is unproven, indeed unsupported. First, there's a big gap between cause and effect—nine months, to be exact. Second, you have no knowledge of the sequence of biological processes that link intercourse and pregnancy, no knowledge of the causal chain. Third, the cause and the effect are very different in scale and duration. And fourth, many other factors that may correlate with intercourse are difficult to rule out—for example, sitting under a palm tree and holding hands in full moonlight (an explanation once advanced in a letter to "Dear Abby").

There is only one way to settle the issue and save the tribe from extinction: conduct an experiment. From a sample of 200 couples, you assign 100 to test intercourse and 100 to test nonintercourse. After some time, you get the following results: of the 100 couples assigned to test intercourse, 20 became pregnant and 80 did not; of the 100 assigned to test nonintercourse, 5 became pregnant and 95 did not. (These five pregnancies represent a fairly typical measurement error in such data and can be explained by faulty memory, lying, and human frailty.)

With the results in hand, you calculate the correlation between intercourse and pregnancy and find that it is .34. Since this correlation is only modest, you conclude that intercourse is not a major factor in causing pregnancy. You discard your unsupported theory and press on for another solution. Could there be something to that palm tree theory, after all?

Three steps back

This example illustrates the three interrelated phases of thinking backward: finding relevant variables, linking them in a causal chain, and assessing the plausibility of the chain.

The search for an explanation often begins when we notice that something is different, unusual, or wrong. Usually, it takes an unexpected event to pique our curiosity—we are rarely interested in finding out why we feel "average" or why traffic is flowing "normally." In the case of our cave dwellers, the declining birthrate is both unusual and threatening and therefore stimulates remedial action.

The next step is to look for some relevant causal factor, to focus on some abnormal event that resembles the unusual outcome in a number of ways: it may be similar in scale, in how long it lasts, or in when it happens. Most people harbor the notion that similar causes have similar effects. For example, according to "the doctrine of signatures," adopted in early Western medicine, diseases are caused or cured by substances that physically resemble them. Thus, a cure for jaundice would be yellow, and so on. As strange as that

may seem, it is also difficult to imagine how we could search for variables without looking for some kind of similarity between cause and effect.

The search for similarity often involves analogy and metaphor. In trying to understand how the brain works, for instance, we can imagine it as a computer, a muscle, or a sponge. Each metaphor suggests a different way of picturing the brain's processes. A computer suggests information input, storage, retrieval, and computation. A muscle suggests building power through use and loss of strength because of atrophy or the strain of overuse. A sponge suggests the passive absorption of information. The metaphor we choose in describing the brain—or in understanding any link between cause and effect—is critical since it directs attention to one way of thinking.

The search for causally relevant variables goes hand in hand with the consideration of indicators, or "cues to causality," that suggest some probable link between cause and effect. There are four categories of cues: temporal order (causes happen before effects), proximity (causes are generally close to effects in time and space), correlation (causes tend to vary along with effects), and similarity (causes may resemble effects through analogy and metaphor or in length and strength).

These cues to causality do not necessarily prove a link between cause and effect. They do, however, indicate likely directions in which to seek relevant variables and limit the number of scenarios or chains that can be constructed between possible causes and their supposed effects.

How likely is it, for example, that sunspots cause price changes on the stock market? Before you dismiss this as an absurd hypothesis, consider that the eminent nineteenth-century economist William Stanley Jevons believed in such a link. To make this link, you have to construct a causal chain that meets various constraints. For the sake of discussion, let's assume that at a certain time some sunspots did occur before price changes (the temporal order is correct); that when the sun had sunspot activity, there were many price changes (the correlation is positive); and that these price changes occurred six months after sunspot activity (the proximity in time is not very close). The task is to bridge the time lag and distance gap between sunspots and price changes. If you cannot do so, you cannot prove a causal relationship.

Now consider the following chain: sunspots affect weather conditions, which affect agricultural production, which affects economic conditions, which affect profits, which affect stock prices. The cues to causality constrain the possible chains that you can imagine. This constraint is especially important in evaluating the cue of temporal order: for one event to cause another, it must precede it. But the cues of proximity in time and space, of congruity, and of the length and strength of cause and effect also constrain the linkage. The way to bridge the spatial and temporal gaps between the sunspots and the stock market changes is to look for a change in the weather.

Imagine, however, that price changes occur immediately after sunspot activity rather than six months later. The closeness in time between the two events eliminates the link between weather and these economic conditions, which requires a time delay. To link sunspots and price changes, you would have to come up with another scenario that meets the test of proximity in time.

Another test that the cues to causality suggest is incongruity–that is, small causes that yield big effects or big causes that produce small effects. To account for these apparent discrepancies, the causal chain must involve some kind of amplification in the first case and some sort of reduction in the second. When Louis Pasteur advanced the germ theory of disease in the 1800s, for example, it must have seemed incredible to his contemporaries, solely because of the test of incongruity. How could tiny, invisible creatures cause disease, plague, and death? In the absence of scientific information, people saw no causal chain that could amplify such minute causes to such enormous effects.

Better thinking backward

Several approaches can improve the way we make thinking backward work in decision making:

1   **Use several metaphors.** Because backward thinking is both intuitive and swift, most people can generate a single metaphor quickly and expand it into an extensive causal chain. But all metaphors are imperfect. When you use them, it is important to remember the old adage that the map is not the territory.

Using several metaphors can be a guard against prematurely adopting a single model. Instead of focusing on one metaphor, experiment with several. Consider, for example, how you might think about complex organizations such as graduate schools of business. Each metaphor illuminates a different dimension of the subject. You could think of business schools as finishing schools, where students mature appropriately before entering corporate life; as military academies, where students prepare for economic warfare; as monasteries, where students receive indoctrination in economic theology; as diploma mills, where students receive certification; or as job shops, where students are tooled to perform specific tasks.

Each metaphor illustrates a different factor, an alternative way of thinking. No metaphor by

itself is adequate; considering them all provides a more complete picture.

2   **Do not rely on one cue alone.** Inferring causality from just one cue often leads to serious error. Because they relied on a single measure, the cave dwellers diverted their attention from the real cause of pregnancy. Correlation does not always imply causation, nor does causation always imply correlation.

3   **Sometimes go against the cues.** A great benefit of the cues is that they give structure to our perceptions and help us interpret ambiguous information. But there is a trade-off between this structure and novelty and originality. The cues help by directing attention to what is obvious and reducing alternative interpretations. But the hallmark of insights is that they surprise us. One way to promote creative thinking, then, is to go against the cues. When searching for an explanation for a complex outcome, sometimes look for a simple or a dissimilar cause rather than a complex or a similar one.

4   **Assess causal chains.** The way to test potential causes and effects is through a causal chain, but the strength of each chain varies. The chain connecting sunspots and stock prices, for instance, is weak because there are so many links and each is uncertain. In fact, most causal chains are only as strong as their weakest links, and long chains are generally weaker than short ones. But research indicates that people do not always grasp these facts. Many people regard complex scenarios with detailed outcomes as much more coherent– and thus much more likely–than simple ones. It is important to evaluate chains according to the number and strength of their links.

5   **Generate and test alternative explanations.** Most people have a natural aptitude for thinking diagnostically. But one of its drawbacks is that it can lead to superstitions that hold sway for long periods. The history of medicine is full of them. For many years, doctors used bloodletting, for instance, as a popular and presumably scientifically sound cure. Could our most cherished theories about economics and business in time become as obsolete as bloodletting?

Experiments can guard against superstition. To assess the effectiveness of advertising, for example, you could conduct experiments by stopping advertising completely. If it is not feasible to go to such extremes, you could use partial tests, which can give you much useful information: you could stop advertising only in certain areas or for certain periods.

If you can't do such an experiment, you can nevertheless imagine situations in which the effect occurs without the suspected cause. In imaginary scenarios, you can judge causal links. The question under consideration may be whether a particular advertising campaign has caused an increase in sales. By trying to answer the question, Would sales have risen without the advertising campaign? you can get an esti-

"Well, it so happens I've diversified. I'm now the hobgoblins of big and medium as well *as little minds."*

mate of the proper link between sales and advertising. A worthwhile experiment would include a second question: Will sales go up if we advertise? By posing these questions in a systematic way, you can get information almost as useful and powerful as what you get from actually trying something out.

Thinking forward

Whether we like to acknowledge it or not, most of the time we do a poor job of thinking forward with any accuracy. Evidence gathered in such diverse fields as marriage counseling, bank lending, economic forecasting, and psychological counseling indicates that most human predictions are less accurate than even the simplest statistical models.

Most people have more faith in human judgment, however, than in statistical models. The disadvantages of statistical models compared with human judgment seem obvious. Or so the argument goes. But is this right? Let's consider the evidence.

Models make errors. The use of a formal model implies trade-offs; a model will make errors since it is an abstraction that cannot possibly capture the full richness of the relations between variables. Human judgment, on the other hand, can sometimes capitalize on idiosyncratic features that are difficult or impossible to model.

Human judgment can also result in errors, but models are perfectly consistent; they never get bored, tired, or distracted, as people do. Models are never inconsistent or random—in fact, they may be consistent to a fault. The important question, then, is which method leads to less overall error.

Or to put the question another way, if we accept the inevitability of some error from using a formal model, will we end up with less overall error by using the model rather than human judgment? According to the results of psychological experiments on probability learning, the answer is yes.

In these studies, subjects are asked to predict which of two lights—one red, one green—will go on. If they guess right, the subjects get a cash reward. If they guess wrong, they get no reward. A random process governs which light goes on, but by arrangement, the red light goes on 60% of the time and the green light, 40%. Subjects are not told about the percentages but have the opportunity to learn about them by participating in the experiment.

The result of this kind of experiment is something called probability matching: subjects learn to respond to cues in the same proportion as they occur. In this case, subjects predict red about 60% of the time and green, 40%. And yet they do not come up with the best predictive strategy that will gain the greatest cash reward, because they are unwilling to accept error.

By predicting red 60% of the time and green 40%, subjects can expect to be right a total of 52% of the time: they will be right on the red light 36% of the time and right on the green light 16% of the time.

But what would happen if subjects were willing to predict red, the more likely color, every time? Such a strategy accepts error; it also leads to 60% correct prediction—8% higher than a strategy that seeks the right answer on every guess.

The subjects would make more money if they accepted error and consistently used a simple mathematical model. Most subjects try to predict perfectly, though, and futilely attempt to discern some nonexistent rule or pattern that determines which light will go on. Any similarity between this example and playing the stock market is purely coincidental.

Models are static. This criticism is simply not true. Models can and should be updated with new information as it becomes available. Models are now being developed that learn from the outcomes of predicted events. This work, while still in its early stages, suggests models can learn from experience.

As far as human judgment is concerned, it is simply not clear that people do learn from feedback in making predictions. Part of the difficulty in learning occurs when people make predictive judgments to take action. The outcomes provide only ambiguous feedback on the quality of the predictions.

For example, imagine a case in which the president of the United States takes strong measures to counteract a predicted economic slowdown. Now consider the difficulties of learning from the various possible outcomes. Imagine having no recession as an outcome. This could result either from an incorrect prediction and an ineffective action or from an accurate prediction and a highly effective action. Now imagine a recession as an outcome. This could result either from an accurate prediction and an ineffective action or from an inaccurate prediction and a boomerang action that causes the very malady it is intended to prevent. The problem is this: to learn about our predictive ability requires separating the quality of predictions from the effects of actions based on those predictions.

Models are not worth their cost. In general, it is impossible to evaluate the argument that any marginal increase in accuracy from using models does not outweigh the extra cost of building them. If a model is used to make enough predictions, however, even small increases in accuracy can produce large benefits.

For example, in the late 1970s, AT&T conducted a study to determine the characteristics of good and bad credit risks.[1] Management incorporated the results in a set of decision rules that it used to determine which new customers should be required to provide deposits. In developing these rules, AT&T went through a time when it granted credit to customers it would have previously classified as both good risks and bad risks. As a result, the rules were validated across the whole range of customer characteristics. By implementing the decision rules, management realized an estimated annual reduction of $137 million in bad debts. While no figures are available on the cost of creating and maintaining the model, it is difficult to believe that the savings did not warrant the expense.

While many phenomena we try to predict are complex, the rules for reasoning forward need not match this complexity. Many successful applications have involved simple combinations of just a few variables. Sometimes the rules develop from modeling an expert's past judgments, sometimes simply by averaging past decisions, and sometimes just by aggregating a few relevant variables.

Backward & forward

Our everyday experience is filled with examples of thinking backward and thinking forward. We are constantly using both modes of reasoning, separately and together, and we are constantly confounded in our efforts.

While explicit rules or models are the best tools to use for reasoning forward, intuition or notions of cause can often exert a powerful influence on the predictions we make. When people take actions in situations where random processes produce the outcomes, they are sometimes subject to delusions of control. For instance, people tend to believe that lottery tickets they personally select have a greater chance of winning than those selected for them by a lottery administrator.

By the same token, in complex situations, we may rely too heavily on planning and forecasting and underestimate the importance of random factors in the environment. That reliance can also lead to delusions of control. The best posture is to remain skeptical toward all undocumented claims of predictive accuracy, whether they are derived from experts, models, or both. Remember the seersucker theory of prediction: for every seer, there is a sucker.[2]

An important paper on how to improve predictive ability once expressed the task of thinking forward in this way: "The whole trick is to decide what variables to look at and then know how to add."[3] But "the trick" is a difficult one that requires complex thinking backward. Indeed, computer scientists who are working to build programs that simulate the understanding process by means of artificial intelligence have had great difficulty in modeling this process. A recent example concerns a program they wrote to simulate the comprehension of newspaper headlines. They provided the program with background knowledge and a set of rules to rewrite the headlines. One such headline was: "World shaken. Pope shot." The computer interpreted this as: "Earthquake in Italy. One dead."

Although the psychological study of judgment and decision making has concentrated on separating thinking backward from thinking forward by clarifying the distinction, the two modes of reasoning are interdependent. Like the god Janus in Roman mythology, whose head has two faces, one facing forward, the other backward, our thinking goes in both directions whenever we put our minds to work on making a decision. ▽

1 J.L. Showers and L.M. Chakrin, "Reducing Uncollectible Revenue from Residential Telephone Customers," *Interfaces*, December 1981, p. 21.

2 J. Scott Armstrong, *Long-Range Forecasting* (New York: Wiley, 1978).

3 Robyn M. Dawes and Bernard Corrigan, "Linear Models in Decision Making," *Psychological Bulletin*, February 1974, p. 95.

Reprint 87107

Can You Analyze This Problem?

A management exercise

By Perrin Stryker

The ability of managers to solve problems and make decisions rationally has long been assumed to be one of the valuable products of experience on the job. But close observation of their actual practices has shown that even veteran managers are likely to be very unsystematic when dealing with problems and decisions. And their hit-or-miss methods often produce decisions based on erroneous conclusions, which means that the decisions must also be wrong.

Some years ago, the surprisingly inefficient ways in which managers use information led Charles H. Kepner, a social psychologist, and Benjamin B. Tregoe, a sociologist, to develop a systematic approach to problem solving and decision making. A description of the research and training methods developed by Kepner-Tregoe and Associates of Princeton, N.J., was presented to HBR readers in an earlier issue.[1] And by now more than 15,000 experienced managers in major corporations have been trained in their concepts of problem analysis and decision making. These concepts are shortly to be published in book form.[2]

Practically every manager who has taken this training has been rather rudely shocked to discover how faulty his or her own reasoning methods have been in handling problems and

decisions. Readers are therefore invited to test their own reasoning powers against the problems presented in the case history, based directly on an actual situation, set forth below.

The Burred Panels

The problems to be solved are presented in the form of dialogues between various managers in a plant which manufactures quarter panels — the body parts that cover the front quarters of the car, including the wheels. The quarter panel is the successor to the fender, and is the part most often damaged in collisions in traffic accidents. This plant has 3,000 employees and makes not only quarter panels but many other smaller parts and components for two of the models sold by one of the Big Three auto companies.

The panels are made on four separate production lines, each line headed by a huge hydraulic press that stamps the panels out of sheet-steel blanks. When the flat steel arrives at the plant from various suppliers by rail, it is unloaded and carried to a machine which cuts identical-size blanks for all four hydraulic presses. Blanks go to the presses by forklift trucks in pallet stacks of 40 each, and the schedule is so arranged that there is always a supply on hand when the presses are started up on the morning shift.

The Principals

Since this problem, like any other management problem, involves different types of peo-

[1] See "Developing Decision Makers," HBR September–October 1960, p. 115.

[2] Charles H. Kepner and Benjamin B. Tregoe, *The Rational Manager*, edited with an introduction by Perrin Stryker (New York, McGraw-Hill Book Company, Inc.).

ple, the following brief descriptions of the characters, whose names have been disguised, may be useful:

- *Oscar Burger, Plant Manager — a tough manager in his late fifties; known for his willingness to listen to others; considered antiunion by the employees.*

- *Robert Polk, Production Chief — a hard-nosed driver, very able technically, but quick-tongued and inclined to favor certain subordinates; also considered antiunion by the employees.*

- *Ben Peters, Quality Control Manager — reserved, quiet, and cautious when dealing with others; extremely confident in his figures.*

- *Ruth Coggin, Industrial Relations Manager — a fairly typical personnel manager; sympathetic to employees; relies on human relations techniques in dealing with the union.*

- *Andy Patella, Shop Steward — antagonistic to management and eager to prove his power; has developed rapport with Industrial Relations Manager Coggin.*

- *George Adams, Supervisor on Line #1 — steady, solid, and well respected by his line crew.*

- *James Farrell, Supervisor on Line #2 — irrascible, ambitious, and somewhat puritanical; very antiunion.*

- *Henry Dawson, Supervisor on Line #3 — patient, warmhearted, and genuinely liked by his subordinates.*

- *Otto Henschel, Supervisor on Line #4 — aloof, cool, and a bit ponderous; neither liked nor disliked by his crew.*

Morning Emergency

The situation opens at 11:00 a.m. on a Wednesday in the office of Plant Manager Oscar Burger, who has called an emergency meeting. Fifty minutes ago he learned from Production Chief Bob Polk that nearly 10% of the panels coming off lines #1 and #2 were being rejected by Quality Control because of burrs and other rough spots.

BURGER: I've called you in here because we're in real trouble if we can't lick this reject problem fast. The company needs all the panels we can ship, and more, if it's going to catch up with this new-model market. Both new models of the Panther and the Cheetah are going over big, and if we slow down on panels, Detroit will be on my neck fast. So let's get all the facts out on the table and run this thing down before lunch. Bob here tells me Line #1 started putting out rejects about three minutes after the end of the 10 o'clock relief break and Line #2 went wild about 9:30. Bob, suppose you tell us just what you've found out so far.

POLK: You've about covered it, Oscar. Farrell, the supervisor now on Line #2, says he's checked several times to see if these burrs in the panels are being caused by something in the sheets, but he hasn't found anything suspicious. Sheets all look nice and clean going into the press, but many come out rough as hell. He says the inspectors report that rejects rose from the normal one or two an hour to eight or nine in the last hour. On Line #1, George Adams says it's about the same story, and he can't figure it out — it just started up suddenly after the relief break.

BURGER: Doesn't Farrell or Adams have *any* idea why it started?

POLK: Well, Farrell is sure it's deliberate sabotage by the drawpress operators, but he can't catch them at it. He says it's not hard to produce burrs and rough spots if an operator positions a sheet just slightly wrong. He says the operators on his line are mad as hell over his suspending Joe Valenti yesterday, and he had another argument when Valenti came in this morning against orders and tried to take back his press job. Farrell called the guard and had Valenti escorted to the gate.

BURGER: What's that? I never heard about this. What's wrong with Valenti? (*He turns to Industrial Relations Manager Coggin.*) Ruth, what about this?

COGGIN: Oh, I don't think it's all Valenti's fault. He and Farrell have been at it for a long time, as you no doubt know, arguing over management's rights. Farrell says he saw Valenti go behind the tool crib yesterday afternoon during the relief break, and Farrell swears Valenti had a bottle with him. He caught Valenti drinking on the job last year, you remember, and says he wishes he'd fired Valenti then instead of suspending him. You know how Farrell is about liquor, especially on the job. Anyway, he accused Valenti of drinking on the job again, and after some hot words he sent Valenti home for the rest of the week. Andy Patella, the

shop steward, protested Farrell's action immediately, of course.

POLK: Farrell's OK, Ruth, he's doing his job.

BURGER: Let's get back to this reject problem.
What has Valenti got to do with it?

COGGIN: Well, I talked with Patella, and he
reports the workers on all four lines are mad.
They made some sharp cracks about
Farrell being a union-buster yesterday after
the argument and again this morning when
he threw Valenti out. When the drawpress
on #2 started putting out a lot of rejects on
Panther panels, and Quality Control reported
this to Farrell, he went over to the press operator and made some suggestions on placing the
sheets, or something like that. The man just
glared at him and said nothing, Patella tells me,
and Farrell finally walked away. The reject
rate stayed high, and during the whole 15
minutes of the relief break operators from all
the lines were talking together about Valenti's
case. Patella says Valenti's young brother, Pete,
a spot welder who works on Line #3 under
Dawson, called for a walkout, and quite a few
seemed to think it was a good idea — contract or
no contract. Then right after they went back to
work, Line #1 started to throw off rejects at a
high rate.

BURGER: What does Adams think about this,
Ruth.

COGGIN: He won't completely buy that sabotage theory of Farrell's, but he admits there
doesn't seem to be any other explanation. The
maintenance troubleshooters have been all over
the press and can't find anything wrong. The
die is OK, and the hydraulic system is OK. They
made some adjustments on the iron claw that
removes the piece from the press, but that's all.

BURGER (turning to Quality Control Manager
Ben Peters): Ben, what is your idea about this?

PETERS: It's hard to say what might be causing
it. We've been checking the sheets from Zenith
Metals we started using this morning, and they
looked perfect going through the blanker. Besides, it's only on lines #1 and #2 that we're
getting burrs, so maybe we've got trouble with
those presses.

POLK: I'll check it with Engineering, but I'm
willing to bet my last dollar the presses are OK.

BURGER: Yes, I think you can forget about
trouble in the presses, Ben. And the blanker's
never given us a hard time, ever. Still, you'd
better have Engineering check that too, Bob,
just in case. Meanwhile, I'd like to . . . . (He
pauses while the door opens and Burger's secretary slips in and hands Peters a note.)

PETERS: I'll be damned! My assistant, Gerrie,
tells me that Line #4 has just begun turning out
a mess of burred rejects. I wouldn't have
thought that slow old line could go haywire
like that — those high-speed presses on the
other lines, maybe, but not on Henschel's steady
old #4 rocking along at 50 panels an hour.

POLK: Well, that seems to knock out a theory I
was getting ready to offer. With #4 acting up,
too, it looks like the press speeds aren't to blame.
Now I guess we won't have long to wait before
Dawson's line also starts bugging up the blanks.

COGGIN: Maybe #3 won't go sour if what Patella says about Dawson is true. He says Dawson's crew would go all out for him if he asked
them, and I gather Patella hasn't had much success selling them on his anticompany tactics.

BURGER: What's he peddling now?

COGGIN: Same old stuff. He claims the company is trying to discredit the union with the
workers, especially now that contract negotiations are coming up next month. This year he's
also tossed in the rumor that the company will
threaten to abandon this plant and move out
of the state if the union does not accept the
local package of benefits management offers in
negotiations.

BURGER: That's stupid. Hell, when will the
union wake up and give us a fair day's work
for the pay they're getting? But let's stop this
chatter and get after these rejects. Check anything and everything you can think of. We
can't afford to shut any line down with the fac-
tory as tight as it is on Panther panels. Let's
meet back here at 4 o'clock this afternoon.

Informal Get-Together

*The meeting breaks up, and Polk goes to the
shop floor to check on the presses and the blanker. Peters goes to his quality-control records
to see when the reject rate last hit its current level. Industrial Relations Manager Coggin
seeks out Patella to check on Farrell's handling
of Valenti and the other operators on his line. During*

the lunch hour in the cafeteria, an informal meeting of the four supervisors and Production Chief Bob Polk takes place.

FARRELL: I suppose you got the boss all straightened out on those rejects, Bob. That Valenti has a lot of friends, and we'll need to keep our eyes peeled to actually catch them fouling up the stampings.

HENSCHEL: You can say that again! I've got a couple of Valenti's old pals on my line, and ever since the burrs started showing up about 11:20, they've been extra careful. I've traced at least three rejects that I think I can attribute to him.

POLK: Keep a count on who makes the most rejects, and maybe we can pin this down to a few soreheads.

ADAMS: You all sound like you're on a witch hunt. As for me, I think Engineering will come up with the answer. The press on my line has been making more noise than usual today, and I think there's something fishy there. Right now, Bob, I'd like your help in getting the night shift to cut down on the number of stacks of blanks they leave us for the morning runs. It'd help a lot if they'd keep it down to two stacks of 40 each. Again this morning I had four stacks cluttering up my area.

POLK: I'll see what we can do with Scheduling.

HENSCHEL: I'm with you there, Adams. I've been loaded with four stacks for the last five days running. With my slow-speed old equipment, I could manage nicely with only one stack to start off. I noticed that Farrell had two stacks and Dawson had only one to start his line today, and why should they be getting favors?

DAWSON: Now, Otto, you're just jealous of my new high-speed press. You got an old clunker, and you know it. What you need is to get off that diet of Panther panels and join me banging out those shallow-draw panels for the Cheetah. Also, it might help you to smile now and then when one of your people cracks a joke. Remember that old proverb, "He that despiseth small things shall fall by little and little."

FARRELL: I can think of another proverb that you might consider, Dawson. "Spare the rod and spoil the child." Is it true that your crew

is going to win a trip to Bermuda if they're all good and make nothing but perfect panels?

ADAMS: Aw, cut it, Farrell. We can't all be tough guys.

FARRELL: Well anyway, I'm glad Dawson didn't have to cope with Valenti today. That boozer is finally out of my hair. I can't forget last year when he helped Patella spread the word that if the operaters would burr a lot of the stampings, they could pressure management into a better contract. I wouldn't be surprised if Valenti and Patella were in cahoots now, trying the same angle before negotiations start.

ADAMS: Relax, Farrell. You can't prove that's so. The operators aren't that dumb, as last year proved when they refused to believe Patella. What bugs me is those rejects this morning. Never saw so many bad burrs show up so fast.

HENSCHEL: They sure surprised me, too, but you know I think Quality Control may be a little bit overexcited about the burrs. I figure all of them could be reamed and filed out with a little handwork. Put two extra people on the line, and it would be all taken care of.

FARRELL: Maybe so, but you know how Burger would feel about the extra costs on top of the lower output. And don't forget, Henschel, our high-speed presses are banging out 30 more an hour than yours. Well, I gotta get back and see what's with Valenti's pals on my line.

Aside Conversation

All the supervisors get up and leave together. They pay no attention to Industrial Relations Manager Coggin talking with Shop Steward Patella in a corner of the cafeteria.

COGGIN: What I want to know, Andy, is why did Valenti try to get back on the line this morning against Farrell's orders?

PATELLA: Why not? Farrell was miles off base sending Joe home yesterday without telling me or you or anyone else. I was glad Joe came back and faced that s.o.b. Farrell's been getting jumpier and jumpier lately, and do you know what they say? They say he's cracking up over that poor kid of his — the little teenager who's turned out to be such a tramp. I feel sorry for him, but that's no reason why he has to take his feelings out on his crew. They won't take it much longer, and the other crews are sore, too. You know Valenti's brother this morning over on line #3 began talking about a walkout?

COGGIN: Yes, I heard he did. So why didn't they go out?

PATELLA: Oh, that crew of Dawson's is too company-minded, and there are some older people there who almost worship Dawson. But they'll go out if management doesn't wise up and respect their rights.

COGGIN: What about that man who got hurt last night on overtime while unloading those sheets?

PATELLA: He's been on the job for a couple of months, but he tells me he wasn't familiar with the method of blocking that Zenith Metals uses. He's not hurt bad, but he'll get workmen's compensation OK.

COGGIN: Sure. Now how certain are you about Farrell not finding any bottle behind the tool crib after he suspended Valenti? And are you sure you're right that there were no witnesses? You know you've got to be positive of your evidence.

PATELLA: OK; Ruth. I'm certain, I'm sure, I'm positive!

Afternoon Meeting

Three hours later, Plant Manager Burger is again in a meeting with Production Chief Polk, Quality Control Manager Peters, and Industrial Relations Manager Coggin.

BURGER: Let's hear from you first, Bob, about that check on the presses and the blanker. Any clues to those burrs?

POLK: Nope. Everything is OK with the machinery, according to Engineering. They even thought I was nuts to be questioning them and making them double-check.

BURGER: I can imagine. But we can't overlook anything, no matter how impossible Engineering may think it is. By the way, Ben, are the rejects still running as high this afternoon?

PETERS: Higher. Line #1 is lousing up nine or ten an hour, Line #2 is ruining about a dozen, and Line #4 is burring about seven an hour.

BURGER: What about Line #3?

PETERS: Nothing so far. Dawson's line has been clean as a whistle. But, with Valenti's brother on the line, we can expect trouble any time.

POLK: Maybe not. Dawson's reject rates have always been a bit lower than the others'.

BURGER: That so? How do you account for that?

COGGIN: How about better supervision accounting for it? Dawson's people always seem to take more pride in their work than the other men do, and they really operate as a team. The other day I heard two of them talking about one of their crew who apparently was getting careless, and they decided to straighten him out themselves, without bothering Dawson. When you get that kind of voluntary discipline, you've got real supervision.

BURGER: Glad to hear that some of our people feel responsible for doing good work.

POLK: Dawson's crew is OK. One of them will always tip me off early if they're getting low on blanks, but the night shift on that line is mighty careless. That crew left Dawson's line with only a half-hour's stack of blanks to start up with this morning.

PETERS: By the way, Bob, have you heard that some of the operators on the other crews are calling his men "Dawson's Darlings? The rumor is that those shallow Cheetah panels are easier to make, and someone played favorites when they gave that production run to Dawson's crew.

POLK: That's crazy. We gave those panels to Dawson's line because this makes it easier for the Shipping Department, and they just aren't any easier to make; you know that.

PETERS: I know, but that's what they say, and I thought you'd like to be cut in on the grapevine.

COGGIN: If the operators think the deep panels are a harder job, maybe there's something to it. I've heard this story, too, and there's a chance the union may try to review our rates and standards one of these days.

POLK: Yeah? Well, I say nuts to it. If those items go on the agenda, then Patella might as well be running this shop. Why don't we ask the union: "How about making up for that half-hour Line #2 lost this morning while Valenti argued with Farrell about his suspension?"

COGGIN: While you're asking, ask Farrell why he didn't call me before suspending Valenti yesterday. What a mess Farrell put us in!

BURGER: What do you mean, Ralph?

COGGIN: Just that we've got a real big grievance coming up, for sure. Patella tells me that after Farrell suspended Valenti yesterday, he went looking behind the tool crib and couldn't find any sign of a liquor bottle. Also, Patella claims there were no witnesses around when Farrell accused Valenti of drinking on the job. It's going to be impossible for Farrell to prove he wasn't acting merely on his suspicions, without evidence. And the union is sure to hit us hard with this, especially with contract negotiations coming up.

BURGER: Damn it, Farrell should have known better! This isn't the first time he's been tough with people but he's got to learn to use better judgement. Bob, you'd better have a talk with him right away. See if anything special is chewing him. Maybe a little firm advice from you will sharpen him up.

POLK: OK, Oscar, but Farrell's a very good man, and we ought to back him up on this completely.

COGGIN: If you do, you're going to have real trouble with the union. Patella says if we don't drop the charge against Valenti and reinstate him, he's going to propose a strike vote, and he claims the crews will positively go out. It looks like they have a clear case against Farrell and, except for Dawson's crew, a lot of them seem plenty sore. And those rejects they're producing are telling you so, loud and clear.

POLK: Oscar, we can't undercut Farrell! If we do, we're playing right into the union's hands. It's obvious that Valenti is in collusion with Patella on this, and they're framing Farrell to get themselves a hot issue for the contract negotiations. I say we should charge the union with framing Farrell and willfully producing rejects. If they try to strike, get an injunction immediately so we can keep production up and satisfy Detroit.

BURGER: Not so fast, Bob. I'd rather first try to get the union off our backs before they seri-

ously start talking about a strike. Ruth, what about that demand the local union agent told you they were going to make — something like 10 minutes' extra wash-up time? If we gave in to them on this, do you think they could hold Patella in line on this Farrell-Valenti problem?

COGGIN: Probably. But you would want to find some way for Patella to save face, as well as Farrell.

BURGER: You may be right, but we can't let Patella think he can go on using this sabotage technique of his. I want to mull this over some more before deciding what our answer will have to be. Meanwhile, Ben, you keep a close check on the reject rates. And you, Bob, check on the operation on Line #3 to see if there really is anything to that rumor about our favoring Dawson's crew. Ruth, see what you can find out about that extra wash-up time deal and how Patella feels about it. That's about all I can suggest for now. Let's meet again tomorrow at 10 o'clock and wind this thing up.

Burger's Dilemma

The meeting breaks up and the managers go back to their respective jobs. Plant Manager Burger spends some time alone trying to resolve the dilemma. He sees two choices facing him: (1) back up Farrell and risk a strike that might be stopped by injunction, or (2) avoid a strike by undercutting Farrell, reinstating Valenti, and asking the crews to cooperate in eliminating excess rejects. He does not like either of the alternatives, and hopes he can think of some better way to get out of this jam. At least, he tells himself, he has a night to sleep on it.

Your Analysis?

Has Plant Manager Burger analyzed the situation correctly? You are invited to think through this situation for yourself and decide how you would go about solving it. You will be able to compare your results with the solutions that will be presented in Part II in the July–August issue of HBR, which will describe the Kepner-Tregoe concepts and procedures for problem analysis.

Reprint 65312

How to Analyze That Problem

Part II
of a management exercise

By Perrin Stryker

Part I of this two-installment article on problem analysis, published in the May–June issue of HBR, invited readers to test their reasoning powers against the problems presented in a case history based directly on an actual situation. This case was reported to Kepner-Tregoe and Associates, whose systematic approach to problem analysis, as described in this installment, made possible the correct solution of a very puzzling situation.

Before resuming the action, I will first give a brief synopsis of what has transpired in the first installment and then introduce the characters who appear in this concluding part (all but one of whom appeared in Part I).

The Situation

In a plant making quarter panels and other parts for one of the Big Three auto companies, the Plant Manager and three key subordinates are trying to find out why burrs and rough spots are suddenly appearing on so many panels, causing them to be rejected. They strongly suspect deliberate sabotage by the operators on the production lines, who are reported to be angry over the suspension of worker Joe Valenti by a hot-headed supervisor, who accused him of drinking on the job. The shop steward threatens to call a strike if the supervisor is not reprimanded for his arbitrary action and also if Valenti is not reinstated.

The Plant Manager collects as many facts as possible in a meeting with his key subordinates, and then adjourns the meeting until the next morning. In the meanwhile, he hopes he can decide what to do. He sees two alternatives: back up the supervisor and risk a strike that might be stopped by injunction; or avoid a strike by undercutting the supervisor, reinstating Valenti, and asking the workers on the line to cooperate in eliminating the excessive rejects. The Plant Manager hopes that he can find another, better alternative, however, before the second meeting with his managers.

The Principals

The following short descriptions of the characters who appear in this second part of the article (the names are disguised) may be useful:

- *Oscar Burger, Plant Manager — a tough manager in his late fifties; known for his willingness to listen to others; considered antiunion by the employees.*

- *Robert Polk, Production Chief — a hard-nosed driver, very able technically, but quick-tongued and inclined to favor certain subordinates; also considered antiunion by the employees.*

- *Ben Peters, Quality Control Manager — reserved, quiet, and cautious when dealing with others; extremely confident in his figures.*

- *Ruth Coggin, Industrial Relations Manager — a fairly typical personnel manager; sympathetic to employees; relies on human relations techniques in dealing with the union.*

•*Joyce Luane, Scheduling Supervisor — persistent, analytical, and systematic; has had some training in problem analysis procedure, but lacks experience.*

Problem Analysis

The situation for Part II of this case opens at 9:30 a.m. on Thursday in the office of Plant Manager Burger (the next-morning meeting).

BURGER: Before we begin this morning, you notice I've asked Joyce Luane, our Scheduling Supervisor, to sit in with us. She's just returned from taking a five-day course in problem solving and decision making, and I thought this would be a good chance to see if she's really learned anything. Now then, Ben, let's hear about those reject rates on the panels. How do they look this morning?

PETERS: They're still way over our 2% tolerance on lines #1, #2, and #4. If anything, they're a bit higher than yesterday.

BURGER: Hasn't Line #3 begun to foul up a lot of panels yet?

PETERS: No signs of it, Oscar.

BURGER: Bob, did Engineering check out the stamping press on Line #3? You know we wanted to track down that rumor about the stamping job on the Cheetah panels being easier than on the Panther panels.

POLK: Engineering says it's strictly rumor — there's absolutely no difference in the stamping time required on any of the four lines.

BURGER: Damn . . . I thought that we might have traced this reject trouble to the presses somehow.

COGGIN: You still can't say that the people on lines #1, #2, and #4 don't feel that the work on Dawson's Line #3 is easier; and if they think Dawson's crew has been favored by getting the Cheetah panels, there could be something in it.

BURGER: But Engineering says no, Ruth. We can't psychoanalyze people to find out why they believe this, if they really do. More to the point, what did you find out about that wash-up time deal the local union agent plans to ask us for?

COGGIN: Shop Steward Patella says he'll be glad if the workers get this extra time, but he still demands that Valenti be reinstated and that Supervisor Farrell be reprimanded. I don't think Patella would back down even if the local agent told him not to threaten a strike. And the operators really seem sore enough to walk out on us.

BURGER: All right, then, that settles it. I've made up my mind. Since we've got to avoid a strike at all costs, with Detroit hounding us for all the panels we can ship, we're going to reinstate Valenti, reprimand Farrell, and also jack up the other supervisors so they'll catch any one trying to produce rejects deliberately. Then we'll ask the crews to cooperate in keeping the reject rates within our tolerance. You, Ruth, will tell Patella that if we catch him inciting people to sabotage the production lines by burring a lot of panels — just in the hope of getting a hot issue for the new contract negotiations — then we'll charge him and the union with this before the NLRB. If they threaten us with a strike, we'll get an injunction to carry us at least over the next two months of maximum output.

POLK: I'm real glad to hear you take a strong line on this, Oscar. We've been too soft with that union for a long time, in my opinion. But I don't think you ought to reprimand Farrell and reinstate Valenti. That could hurt all our supervisors.

BURGER: Sorry, but that's it, Bob. Farrell was too rash in suspending Valenti without any evidence. We've got to calm the operators down and stop this damned burring trouble, or we'll have Detroit on our necks, and hard!

COGGIN: I think you're doing just right, and I'm sure the crews on the lines will cooperate in licking this reject problem.

BURGER: I hope so. Anyway, I can't see a better decision at this time. (*He turns to Luane.*) Now, Joyce, how did we do? What do you think of our problem solving and decision making?

LUANE: I can't really say, Mr. Burger, because I'm not at all sure just what the problem is.

BURGER: Well, it started out as a reject problem and then developed into a touchy union situation we've had to handle.

POLK: The basic problem, Joyce, is discipline in the shop. We've been too lax with the operators and too soft with the union.

COGGIN: I'd say the real problem is our need to train the supervisors in their responsibilities. Also, we've got a communications problem if a supervisor like Farrell fails to get the message that he must notify me before taking disciplinary action.

LUANE: Let's see . . . that makes six problems you have mentioned — rejects, union antagonism, shop discipline, lack of supervisory training, low morale, and poor communications.

BURGER: Yes, but you could say they're really all part of one whole problem, as I see it.

LUANE: One whole problem? What's that? From what I heard, it sounds like you've got a mess of problems here.

BURGER: What I mean by the whole problem is managing this entire plant so everything runs on schedule and putting out what Detroit wants. Did they teach you how to solve that kind of problem in your training course?

LUANE: Not exactly. But I did learn the difference between a problem and a decision, and I think some of you have been mixing these two things up, from what I have heard.

Defining the Problem

Let us pause here for a moment and see what these managers have been doing. First, Plant Manager Burger checked on the points of information he'd asked for at the previous meeting, and these satisfied him that he was right in assuming sabotage to be the cause of the high reject rates on the panels. He then made several decisions which he judged capable of taking care of both the reject problem and the labor difficulties.

Some of Burger's decisions seem right to Production Chief Polk, who only disputes Burger's handling of Farrell and Valenti; and all seem right to Industrial Relations Manager Coggin, who accepts Burger's reasoning completely.

Then Scheduling Supervisor Joyce Luane begins to ask some pertinent questions and finds that each manager is using the word "problem" in a different sense, without realizing it. And they have been repeatedly committing the major error in problem solving — namely, jumping to conclusions about the cause of a problem. For

example, Polk says the "basic problem" is lack of discipline in the shop, and he assumes that this problem is the cause of the excessive rejects. On the other hand, Coggin sees one problem as the need for training, which she says is the cause for low morale, and she sees another problem as lack of communications, which she assumes caused Farrell's blunder; while Burger views all these failings and assumed causes as part of one big "problem of managing this entire plant."

These confusions in meaning are apparent to Luane because she has learned to distinguish problems from decisions. She sees any problem as a deviation from some standard or norm of desired performance. And to her a decision is now always a choice among various ways of getting a particular thing done or accomplished. Thus she recognizes that Coggin is really talking about a decision when she says that "our real problem is the need to train supervisors." Similarly, Luane realizes that Burger's "whole problem" is not a mere collection of failures and causes, but a statement describing his responsibility for making decisions as head of the plant. So Luane tries to clarify some of this confusion.

LUANE: I suggest we agree on what we mean by a problem so we can concentrate on that, and not worry right now about any decisions or any causes. The simplest way to solve a problem is to think of it as something that's wrong, that's out of kilter, something we want to fix. If we identify that for sure, then we can begin to look for what caused it; and when we've found the cause, then we can get into decision making, which is choosing the best way to correct the cause.

BURGER: But it isn't that simple, is it? We want to correct a lot of things around here, and they're usually mixed up together.

LUANE: Yes, but you can't work on them all at once, and you can't solve a lot of problems by correcting just one of them.

BURGER: OK, let's go along with Joyce on this, but I personally think there are times when you can solve a lot of problems by solving one key problem.

LUANE: I think you'll find that the key problem is almost always at the end of a chain of other problems and causes. That is, the cause of one problem is itself a problem, and its cause is another problem, and the cause of that other problem is still another problem to be solved, and so on. It's kind of a stair-stepping sequence. Usually, if you correct the *cause* of the *basic* problem in such a sequence, the other problems and their causes will automatically disappear.

POLK: I'll buy that. If we correct the lax discipline in the shop, we'll correct the reject problem and those labor troubles, too.

LUANE: Not necessarily. You've got to be certain they're connected in a problem-cause sequence. It's safer to assume that they're not connected, and then pick the problem that's most important and start analyzing from there.

BURGER: All right, let's pick our most important problem and get on with this. Obviously the high reject rate on those panels is our biggest problem now. If we don't get it solved fast, at the present rate of rejects we'll be fouling up more than 2,500 panels every shift, and we can't stand for that.

POLK: That's for sure, Oscar, but after we jack up the supervisors and the press operators, and get the reject rates back in line, let's not forget to keep pushing for more discipline.

LUANE: Aren't you talking now about a decision, Bob — what should be done to keep things going as you think they should?

POLK: I guess so, by your definition, but it's damned important.

LUANE: I'm not doubting it, but we still haven't decided that the reject problem is our number one problem.

COGGIN: If you mean the biggest immediate problem, then I'll admit it's the rejects, but they're only symptoms of bigger, more fundamental problems, in my opinion.

BURGER: If we flop in delivering our quota of panels in this busy season, we can cost the company such a pile of money it makes me shudder.

LUANE: What if those reject rates on the panels keep rising?

POLK: Say, haven't we got it bad enough? You know that any rejects above 5% are very serious business. We've got to hold them below 2% — no "if"s or "but"s or we can shut up shop.

LUANE: OK, fair enough. I was just trying to make sure we had identified not only the most serious and urgent problem, but the one that could grow into real critical financial trouble.

COGGIN: I'm still convinced that our most important problem has to do with people, especially our headaches in training and helping them communicate.

BURGER: Be realistic, Ruth. If we don't correct this reject problem and produce what's required by Detroit, we may not be around to worry about *any* problems.

LUANE: Let's call this reject problem our number one problem. We can list the others, too, but give them less priority right now. Next, we've got to describe this reject problem precisely, and I mean *precisely*.

POLK: Oh, so they taught you to "define the problem first"? Sounds very familiar. Next you'll be telling us to "get all the facts." I've seen a lot of these step-by-step gimmicks, but I don't believe they really work.

LUANE: Matter of fact, getting all the information would just be a big waste of time. Only some of the facts would be useful to us. That's one reason I want to describe this problem precisely. Another reason is that we're going to use this specification to test any possible causes we find.

Outlining the Specification

Again let us see what these managers have been accomplishing. Luane has stated three basic concepts: a problem is a deviation from some standard of desired performance; a decision is a choice of the best way to correct the cause of a problem; and every problem has only one cause. She also has pointed out the stair-stepping process of going from one problem to its cause, which, in turn, may be a problem to be solved.

But the managers don't pay much attention to these ideas, and Polk clearly misunderstands stair-stepping, for he clings to the conclusion he earlier jumped to — that lax discipline is the cause of several problems. Industrial Relations Manager Coggin thinks "people problems" are fundamentally more important, but she accepts the priority her superiors give to the reject problem. At this point, Luane has tried to get the managers to think in terms of the urgency, seri-

ousness, and growth trend of the problem. Having settled on the reject rate as the most important problem, they now are ready to start analyzing it.

LUANE: How would you describe this reject problem, Bob?

POLK: Why, I'd say the problem is that the reject rates are way out of line.

LUANE: How about you, Mr. Burger?

BURGER: Let's see. I'd say it was too many burred panels.

LUANE: And you, Ben? Haven't heard a peep out of you for some time now.

PETERS: I guess I'd go along with Bob on the reject rates being beyond tolerance.

LUANE: We'll have to get more specific. We're trying to describe this exactly. As an overall description, how about "Excessive rejects from burring on quarter panels"? Anyway, let's write that down for a starter. (*She goes to an easel blackboard and writes these words out.*) Now we have to dissect this problem in detail, getting specific facts about it in four different dimensions – *What, Where, When,* and *Extent.* (*She writes these four words down on the left side of the blackboard.*) What's more, we want to get two sets of facts opposite each of these dimensions — those that describe precisely what the problem Is and those that describe precisely what the problem Is NOT. (*She writes* Is *and* Is NOT *at the top of two columns of blank space.*)

POLK: What's all this for, anyway? Are we drawing a chart or something?

LUANE: Sort of a map. This is the specification worksheet, and the point is to fill the Is column with only those things directly affected by the problem. In the Is NOT column we will put the things that are closely related to the problem but not affected by it. You'll see why we do this in a few minutes.

BURGER: OK, but I hope this doesn't take too long. Sounds kind of detailed to me.

LUANE: It's pretty simple, actually. Under *What,* we can first put down "burrs" as the deviation in this Is column, and "any other complaint" in the Is NOT column, since, as I understand it, there are no other complaints reported on these panels. But we can be more specific here, too. For instance, what did this deviation, "burrs," appear on? Were they on all kinds of panels?

POLK: No, Joyce, just on the Panther panels, not the Cheetah panels.

LUANE: So we can put down, under *What,* the words "Panther panels" in the Is column, and "Cheetah panels" in the Is NOT column. Got the idea?

POLK: I guess so, but it sounds a little too simple to me. Why bother?

LUANE: The point here is we're trying to separate what the problem Is from everything that Is NOT the problem. We're aiming to draw a tight line around the problem, to describe it precisely, and later you'll see how this gives us the clues to the cause of the problem.

POLK: I hope so.

LUANE: Now we do the same thing for this *Where* section of the specification. Where was the deviation seen on the objects affected? Obviously, the burrs appeared on the Panther panels, so we put this down under Is. Also, where in the plant were the burrs observed?

BURGER: So far, only on lines #1, #2, and #4, but with Line #3 expected to go bad any minute.

LUANE: So under Is of this *Where* section we can put "lines #1, #2, and #4," and under Is NOT, we can put "Line #3." Also, we have to fill in the Is NOT opposite the words "Panther panels." Where didn't the burrs appear?

POLK: Nowhere else. We all know that.

LUANE: I know, but we've got to make this specification as accurate as possible. We can put down "other parts" under Is NOT, since we know no other parts were affected.

POLK: I can't see where we're going with all this business.

BURGER: Neither can I, Bob, but let's let her finish.

LUANE: Now we come to the *When* part of this specification. Here we ought to be extra careful and get exact times, if possible. Ben, what times did those reject rates start going up yesterday morning?

PETERS: You mean exactly? (*He consults his papers.*) On Line #2, the first excessive rejects showed up at 9:33 a.m.; on Line #1, they appeared at 10:18; and on Line #4, at 11:23 a.m. From those times on, each of these lines turned out rejects that were far above our tolerance of 2%.

LUANE: That's nice and precise. Can't tell, it may be important, so we'll put the exact times down. Now, how about the Is Not here? There were no burrs at all on lines #1, #2, and #4 before these times, and none at all on Line #3 at any time.

BURGER: I think I begin to see why you use those Is and Is Not columns. It's to put off to one side all the facts you aren't going to think about in solving this problem.

LUANE: No, that's not exactly why, but it will be clear as soon as we finish this specification. This last section, called *Extent,* covers the size of the problem — how big or serious it is, how many items are involved. We can put down "bad burring" and list the percentage of rejects on each line. Now what were those percentages, Ben?

PETERS (*consulting his papers again*): On Line #2, 11% rejects. On Line #1, 17.5%, and on Line #4, 15%. That's according to final counts last night.

LUANE: That leaves us only the Is Not column to fill in here, and this would cover the rejects on Line #3. We can say "Line #3 rejects" here, since they have stayed within the 2% tolerance. Now we've got the specification all filled in.

BURGER: Still looks like a simple collection of facts. Is that all there is to this system?

LUANE: No, Mr. Burger. Now we've got to begin analyzing this specification to dig out the cause of this problem.

POLK: You mean *now* we're finally going to start solving it?

Spotting the Distinction

Here we can briefly review what Luane has done in drawing up this specification. She followed a systematic outline to describe precisely both the problem and what lies outside the problem but is closely related to it. (See EXHIBIT I *for Luane's specification worksheet.) The contrast between the* Is *and the* Is Not *not only draws a boundary around the problem, but strictly limits the amount of information needed for its solution. There is no need to "get all the facts" — only the relevant facts.*

Note that Burger, Polk, and Peters all had different ways of describing the reject problem at first. Also, Burger thinks the specification looks too "detailed," while to Polk it sounds "too simple" at one point. The separation of the Is *and the* Is Not *sounds strange to these managers because, like everyone else, they have learned to think in terms of similarities, not differences. This habit will bother them again a little further on in this problem analysis. Both Burger and Polk are impatient with this specification stage because they haven't yet seen the reasoning behind it.*

A precise specification makes possible two logical steps toward finding possible causes of the problem, and after that, as Luane pointed out, it serves as a testing sheet to identify the most likely cause. Luane now turns to the specification on the board and introduces the managers to the most demanding part of this analytical process.

LUANE: We're ready now to use those contrasts between the Is and the Is Not of this specification. Whatever caused this problem produced *only* those effects we have described on the Is side; so if one thing is affected and another related thing is not, then there must be something distinctive or unique about the thing affected to set it apart from the other. If we know what is distinctive. . . .

BURGER (*interrupting*): I don't see any contrast between "burrs" and "any other complaint" in this specification, but I do see one between "Panther panels" and "Cheetah panels." I begin to get what you're driving at. The Panther panels are affected by the cause; the Cheetah ones aren't. We want to find out what sets the Panther panels apart from the Cheetahs, isn't that it?

LUANE: Yes, you look first for a sharp contrast between the Is and the Is Not, like the one you've spotted. Then we know there must be something distinctive about those Panther panels.

BURGER: Both panels are made from the same steel sheets, so the only way you could distinguish one from the other would be by its shape.

EXHIBIT I. SPECIFICATION WORKSHEET

Deviation: Excessive rejects from burring on quarter panels				
	IS	IS NOT	WHAT IS DISTINCTIVE OF THE _IS_ ?	ANY CHANGE IN THIS ?
WHAT Deviation Object	Burrs Panther panels	Any other complaint Cheetah panels	Deep draw	—
WHERE On object observed	Panther panels Lines #1, #2, & #4	Other parts Line #3	Deep draw	—
WHEN On object observed	Line #2 – 9:33 a.m. Line #1 – 10:18 a.m. Line #4 – 11:23 a.m.	Any burrs before these times on Lines #2, #1, & #4 Line #3 at any time	Stacks of Zenith's blanks began to be used at these times	New alloy in Zenith steel
EXTENT How much How many	Bad burring Line #2 – 11 % rejects Line #1 – 17.5% " Line #4 – 15% "	Line #3 rejects	Reject rates not proportional to involvement in Farrell-Valenti conflict	
POSSIBLE CAUSES FOR TEST	A new alloy in Zenith's sheet steel is causing the excessive burring in the presses			

The Panther panels are a deeper draw than the Cheetah panels.

LUANE: That's a distinction all right. We'll put down "deep draw" as a distinction in this _What_ section of the specification. (_She writes the distinction off to one side of the blackboard._) Now can you see any distinction in the _Where_ section?

BURGER: I don't see any distinction there, like in the first case. Nothing distinctive of "Panther panels" as opposed to "other parts" that I can think of. Then you've got lines #1, #2, and #4 on the Is side and Line #3 on the Is Not side, and these lines are damned similar, except that Line #4 is a slow, old-time press. But that would only distinguish Line #4 from lines #1 and #2, which isn't what you're asking for.

LUANE: No, we don't want a distinction like that, between things that are together on the Is side. We're looking for what sets the Is apart from the Is Not.

POLK: How about saying that Panther panels are distinctive of those three lines on the Is side? Line #3 makes only Cheetah panels, as we said a moment ago.

LUANE: We can put it down if we want to, but it's really a contrast we already have in our specification, and not a distinction. It's the same contrast we have here in the _What_ section between Is and Is Not. What we want is something that really sets lines #1, #2, and #4 apart from Line #3.

POLK: Then the only distinction you have there is that same "deep draw," as we said before.

LUANE: I agree. We'll put it down again in this _Where_ section. Let's go and see what distinction we can find in the _When_ section, where we put down the different times that the burrs showed up on lines #1, #2, and #4.

POLK: How about saying those times are all distinctly in the morning, not the afternoon?

LUANE: But how does that make them distinct from Line #3, where there are no times given at all? We're looking for something distinctive associated with those times.

PETERS: Wait a minute! I've got a hunch those times have something to do with the stacks of blanks delivered to the presses. I remember Adams on Line #1 told me late yesterday that the bad burrs began on his line just after using up the four stacks of blanks his area had been loaded with in the morning. And another thing — maybe those high-speed presses are just right for the shallow-draw panel that Dawson's line is stamping, but not quite right for the deep-draw Panther panels.

POLK: Come on, Ben, slow down! You know Henschel's Line #4 has an old, slow press, and he's getting a lot of burrs, so the speed can't be causing the rejects.

PETERS: Not just the speed, Bob, but the speed in combination with the deep-draw panels.

LUANE: Let's stick to this specification job and not jump to conclusions. I'm not knocking your hunches, Ben, for I've found they can often be useful, providing you hold them aside until you start looking for possible causes. We can make a note of them so we won't forget them later. (*He writes off to one side of the specification, "Burring times connected with using up the stacks of blanks," and "Press speed and deep draw combine to make burrs."*)

POLK: I don't think Ben's hunch on press speeds and draws is any good, in any case. Engineering told me a while ago that they spent a lot of time examining the presses at various speeds and never found any stamping defects traceable either to press speeds or to the depth of draw.

PETERS: But how about the combination of speeds and different draws? Bob, I think you've got too much confidence in Engineering.

LUANE: Can we get back to this specification? Does anyone see any distinction in this *When* section?

BURGER: I think Ben has a point there about the stacks of blanks on Line #1 being used up just before the bad burring started. How about the other lines?

PETERS: I don't know, but we can find out.

LUANE: Will it take long?

PETERS: No, just a phone call. (*He reaches for the phone, gets his assistant on the line, and asks her to check the times when lines #2 and #4 used up the stacks of blanks they started out with the morning before.*)

LUANE: While we're waiting, let's look for distinctions in this last section of *Extent*.

POLK: Don't see any, unless it's that "deep-draw" distinction again.

LUANE: As I see it, the distinction would have to be in those rates of burring we put down here, not in the panels or the presses.

BURGER: Well, you could say that the rates of burring on lines #1, #2, and #4 don't correspond very well with the ways those lines were involved with that Farrell-Valenti quarrel. I mean, Farrell's Line #2 ought to show the most burrs, and actually it shows less than the other two lines.

COGGIN: Maybe the reason is that the operators on lines #1 and #4 are really madder than those on Farrell's line. Maybe Valenti has more friends on the other two lines. You can't distribute and measure feelings with percentage points, like you can with those reject figures.

LUANE: Sorry to have to remind you again, Ruth, but that's jumping to a conclusion about the cause. We'd better not do this until we've finished with this specification.

COGGIN: Well, I can't just sit here and let the rest of you ignore the human side of this problem. When are we going to get to that, anyway?

LUANE: We'll take it up if this analysis leads us in that direction. It hasn't yet. So let's put down that distinction connected with the different rates of rejects and the different degrees of involvement with the Valenti affair. We can call this distinction, "Reject rates not proportional to involvement in Valenti conflict."

PETERS (*reading a note his assistant has just brought in*): Here are those times we asked for. Line #2 used up its stacks of Tuesday blanks at 9:30 a.m. yesterday, and Line #4 at 11:20 a.m. That checks out, as I thought. The bad burrs started on all these lines just after they started using stacks of blanks delivered to the floor Wednesday morning.

LUANE: Looks like that gives us a distinction for the *When* section. We can call it, "Stacks of Tuesday's blanks used up at these times."

POLK: But how about Line #3? Ben, did your assistant get the time that Dawson's line finished using its supply of Tuesday's blanks?

PETERS: Yes. At 8:30 yesterday morning.

POLK: And no bad burring started on Line #3, so what's the importance of this distinction?

LUANE: We can't tell yet, Bob, but we'll just put it down for now. That seems to complete our distinctions, unless anyone sees any more in this specification. If not, we can proceed to look for the possible causes of this problem.

Seeking the Cause

At this point these managers have presumably collected all the relevant information that describes their problem precisely and have dug out those distinctive things in the Is *facts that are characteristic marks of the problem. But they had trouble spotting the distinctions, as Luane expected. Also, one of them, Peters, introduced a couple of hunches into the discussion, exhibiting a tendency to "feel" that things are connected somehow or are important.*

Note that Luane does not completely discourage such hunches, only recommends they be set aside until later. But note, too, that Peters' reasoning about his first hunch is faulty, as Polk quickly points out, while his second hunch is simply another example of jumping to a conclusion about the cause, as Luane points out. It is Burger who seems to be the sharpest here in spotting a distinction, after stumbling at first. By this time apparently only Industrial Relations Manager Coggin is still interested in the "human side of the problem," as she puts it, but her job is, of course, most directly concerned with this angle.

Luane, by keeping the discussion on the specification, prevents a time-wasting digression. She also warns Polk against prematurely judging the last distinction (about using up Tuesday's blanks) as useless just because it doesn't seem to fit in with another fact in the specification — that is, the absence of serious burrs on Line #3.

Now Luane introduces the managers to a concept that lies at the heart of problem analysis, the concept that the cause of every problem is a change of one kind or another.

LUANE: The distinctions we've gotten out of the specification give us the areas where we can look for possible causes of these burred panels. Let's look for any changes we can find in any of the distinctions. What's new or different in these distinctions? We probably won't find many. Maybe only one.

BURGER: Do you mean any kind of change?

LUANE: No, only those changes which have occurred within one of these areas of distinction, or have had an effect on one of them. We can start with that distinction of "deep draw."

POLK: I can't believe that a change is always the cause of a problem. It can be any little thing, or some goof-off, or bonehead action.

LUANE: Maybe those things go along with the cause, but I think we'll find here that these burred panels are being caused by some change. Also, Mr. Burger, I meant to point out that we don't want to go looking for everything that's changed, or we'll be here all day. There are things changing all over the plant all the time. But what we want to find is any change that's in one of these areas of distinction.

POLK: I'm not convinced, and what's more I don't see anything changed in that "deep draw" distinction. The deep draw is standardized on all three presses making it, and has been for months.

LUANE: OK, so there's no change there. But what about that distinction we were going to check out in the *When* section? What's changed about those "stacks of Tuesday's blanks used up at these times"? Anything new or different about these stacks?

PETERS: Well, the shift from Tuesday's blanks to Wednesday morning's blanks would be a change.

LUANE: That sounds like a real change to me. Wednesday's stacks are the new blanks the lines started to work on just before the burring started.

BURGER: If that's the cause of these rejects, how do you figure it? I can see that if Wednesday's blanks were different in some way from Tuesday's, that might make them the cause of the rejects.

LUANE: Let's hold off on possible causes until we're sure there aren't some more changes in these distinctions.

POLK: I can't see any more changes. I say let's get on with it and start looking for possible causes.

LUANE: OK, if you want to, but are we sure there's not some change connected with that other distinction in the *Extent* section, which we put down as "rates not proportional to involvement in Valenti conflict"?

BURGER: I don't see anything new or different there, unless it's the differences between those rates themselves.

LUANE: I can't either, so let's go ahead and check that possible cause you suggested a moment ago, when you said yesterday's blanks might be the cause of the excessive burrs. But we should test this possible cause, not just rationalize ourselves into accepting it. If this possible cause fails to explain all the facts in this specification — that is, both the facts on the Is side and those on the Is Not side — then we can be sure it's not the actual cause. Because the actual cause would have produced exactly all those things that we put down as Is in the specification, and also would explain those things we put down as Is Not.

BURGER: I assume this is what you meant when you said earlier that the specification would be used in testing the possible causes?

LUANE: That's right. We can start testing against the *What* of the specification by asking, "Does the use of yesterday's blanks explain the fact that the excessive burrs appear on the Panther panels and not on the Cheetah panels?"

POLK: No, of course it doesn't. Line #3 started using Wednesday's blanks even before the other lines did, and it still hasn't produced excessive burrs on the Cheetah panels.

LUANE: Well then, there goes your possible cause. It doesn't fit the first facts in our specification's Is and Is Not. We'll have to toss it out.

BURGER: You mean we've got to find a possible cause that accounts for every fact in this specification?

POLK: That's what she said, Oscar. But now where does this leave us? We've run out of the only change we could find.

LUANE: What this means is that our specification isn't really complete. We must have missed something somewhere. We'll have to go back and sharpen up our facts if we can.

Respecifying the Problem

We can pause briefly here to point out that Luane herself was responsible for the unsatisfactory results of this first search for the cause of the problem. When she accepted the change that Burger suggested — that is, the change to Wednesday's blanks just before the bad burring started — Luane didn't think to ask about the difference between Tuesday's and Wednesday's blanks. A shift from one day's blanks to another's is not a change if the blanks are identical. Polk saw this at once, of course, and torpedoed this possible cause, as he should have. But this error of Luane's might not have occurred if she had been more careful earlier, as we shall now see.

LUANE: We can go back and look over our Is and Is Not facts in the specification, but these look pretty accurate and precise to me. I think we probably missed a distinction or change.

PETERS: What about those hunches of mine? You said we might come back to them.

LUANE: That's an idea. What was it you said? We wrote them down over here somewhere. Here's one, "Press speed and deep draw combine to make burrs."

POLK: That's no good, as I said before. Engineering checked that thoroughly.

LUANE: Well, here's Ben's other hunch, "Burring times connected with using up the stacks of blanks."

BURGER: We just tested that one out and got nowhere.

PETERS: Hold everything! I think we skipped a point. We talked about yesterday's blanks, but those aren't just yesterday's blanks — they're also blanks from a new supplier, Zenith. I missed this point because we'd made some parts with the Zenith metal before we ever put it in production, and it worked fine. Besides, Zenith's metal met all our specifications. We checked the blanks again when the excessive burring first occurred yesterday, and they looked perfect going through the blanker. So we dropped this as a possibility, especially when the labor trouble looked so hot.

LUANE: Then that means we should change that distinction in the *When* section of our specification to "Stacks of *Zenith's* blanks began to be used at these times."

POLK: How will that help? Dawson's Line #3 is also using Zenith blanks, and there's no burring there.

LUANE: That's jumping to a conclusion about the cause. Let's look for a change in this revised distinction. Is there anything new or different about Zenith's sheet steel? How long have we been using it?

POLK: We signed the contract a month ago.

PETERS: Yes, but we didn't get delivery right off. The first shipment didn't actually get here until two days ago.

COGGIN: Matter of fact, Ben, we didn't get those Zenith sheets until late Tuesday. I know, because one of the men got hurt unloading them that evening. He wasn't familiar with the way Zenith blocks the sheets for shipment.

LUANE: Let's concentrate on what's new or different in Zenith's sheets.

PETERS: I think they're just the same as we got from our other sheet-steel suppliers.

LUANE: Are you sure?

PETERS: Pretty sure. We specified a slightly different alloy for Zenith's sheets, but not enough different to matter.

LUANE: Well, anyway, the new alloy is a change in an area of distinction. What is distinctive about those burring times is that stacks of new metal began being used then, and the change here is that a slightly different metal is going into the presses. We can state the possible cause this way — "A new alloy in Zenith's sheet steel is causing the excessive burring in the presses."

BURGER: Ben just said he thinks the alloy change wasn't enough to matter.

LUANE: I know he did, but it was a change in an area of distinction, so it's a possible cause. We can test it against the facts in the specification. Could this change — the slightly different alloy — explain the appearance of excessive burrs in the Panther panels, but not in the Cheetah panels?

COGGIN: No, it couldn't, because the Cheetah panels aren't having trouble with excessive burrs.

POLK: Hold it a moment! Maybe the alloy could explain it. It just dawned on me that Engineering did say something about those Cheetah panels a couple of months back. Something about how their shallow draw would make it easier to use a tougher alloy in the blanks. That could mean the Panther panels are fouling up on these Zenith blanks with the new alloy! Let's check it! (*He picks up the phone and calls Engineering, which immediately confirms his hypothesis.*) Engineering says the new alloy in the Zenith sheets makes the Panther panels much more likely to burr than the Cheetah panels.

LUANE: Looks like you've found it, Bob. We could go on and test this out against the rest of the specification, but I'd say you've probably discovered the most likely cause of the excessive burrs. I suggest you have Engineering verify this.

POLK: That's easy. We can do it before lunch right on the lines.

BURGER: What if we find this "most likely cause" isn't the answer?

LUANE: Then we'll have to respecify all over again, sharpen up the facts even more, and look for other distinctions and changes. But it looks like we've really spotted the change that's causing the trouble. In this case, the new alloy is the change, the metal supplied by Zenith is the distinction, and the deep draw on lines #1, #2, and #4 is another, added distinction. In other words, the most likely cause turned out to be a change *in* a distinction *plus* a distinction.

COGGIN: You mean, Joyce, we've got to go through this whole business every time in order to solve every problem?

LUANE: If you don't know the cause of the problem for sure, I'd say yes. There may be some times when you can spot a change in some facts about a problem right off and hit the cause at once. Sometimes you can just go through the process mentally, for it tells you the relevant questions to ask about every problem. But you'd better check any possible cause out carefully, and you really can't check completely unless you have a complete specification of the problem in front of you. If you don't check a possible cause this way, you may be taking action on something that's not the cause at all, and waste more time than if you had specified and analyzed the problem in the first place.

BURGER: Sounds logical enough. But what if you can't find a distinction or change?

LUANE: If you can't find any distinction or change in your specification, then you have to dig that much harder. And at least you know where to probe. A distinction *has* to be there if the problem exists, because whatever went wrong affected some things in a certain way, and did not affect other closely related things. There's got to be at least one distinction between these two kinds of things — the Is and the Is NOT — and there's *got* to be a change that works through this area of distinction to cause the problem.

BURGER: I see what you mean. Anyway, if Engineering can verify this alloy change in Zenith's sheets as the cause of those excessive rejects, I'll be damned glad. My face would sure have been red if we went ahead with those decisions I came in here with this morning, all based on the assumption that the operators were to blame for the high reject rates! And it all seemed so reasonable! Now, if this alloy change is actually the cause, all we'll have to do is shift back to sheets with the old alloy formula.

COGGIN: But there's still that labor problem we haven't touched yet. When do we get around to analyzing that Farrell-Valenti trouble for a solution? And we've still got to calm Patella down somehow.

POLK: I think those problems don't need to be analyzed. We know what touched off the Farrell-Valenti trouble; we know why Patella is giving us trouble. What's got to be done now is to make some decisions. All that's needed is some straight talk. Tell the crews the facts and to get on with the job, and tell Patella to pipe down or you'll report him for attempted sabotage.

BURGER: Wait a minute, Bob. Maybe we'd better first try to analyze that Farrell-Valenti trouble a little more systematically. There could be something else to it. Joyce, why not take

a crack at it and then let me know what you come up with? Meanwhile, Bob, you'd better make some arrangements to start reclaiming those rejects as fast as possible. We'll need them all if Detroit asks us for what I think they will.

The meeting ends with Burger and Polk leaving together, the others following them out.

Conclusion

In these concluding exchanges we see that the analysis has clearly uncovered a cause which none of the managers were thinking of when they began, and which was actually verified as the cause. Note that the clue to the change that caused the trouble did not appear until Luane went back to the specification and sharpened up one of the distinctions. It was the point about Zenith's steel sheets that finally jogged Polk into recalling the possible effects of a deep draw on blanks made of the new alloy. Had Luane been more expert in the Kepner-Tregoe analysis procedure, the respecification might not have been necessary.

As it was, this solution turned out to be one of the more difficult kinds — for it involved, as Luane pointed out, a change in a distinction *plus* a second distinction. This second distinction was an essential condition (the deep draw) that had to occur before the particular change (the new alloy) could take effect and burr the panels.

Without a precise specification and careful analysis, only time-wasting guesswork and luck could have arrived at the most likely explanation of this problem. More important, this analysis prevented the Plant Manager from taking action that could have produced a more serious problem than the one he was trying to solve. Also, it should be noted that the managers did not automatically become expert problem-analyzers in going through this experience. They are still likely to jump to conclusions, as Polk did toward the end when he quickly prescribed actions to be taken on Coggin's labor problems without knowing their causes. It takes time to change a manager's thinking habits into a systematic approach to problem analysis.

Reprint 65412

Sherlock Holmes: "It's quite a three-pipe problem."

— Sir Arthur Conan Doyle

Saul W. Gellerman

Why 'good' managers make bad ethical choices

How could top-level executives at the Manville Corporation have suppressed evidence for decades that proved that asbestos inhalation was killing their own employees?

What could have driven the managers of Continental Illinois Bank to pursue a course of action that threatened to bankrupt the institution, ruined its reputation, and cost thousands of innocent employees and investors their jobs and their savings?

Why did managers at E.F. Hutton find themselves pleading guilty to 2,000 counts of mail and wire fraud, accepting a fine of $2 million, and putting up an $8 million fund for restitution to the 400 banks that the company had systematically bilked?

How can we explain the misbehavior that took place in these organizations – or in any of the others, public and private, that litter our newspapers' front pages: workers at a defense contractor who accused their superiors of falsifying time cards; alleged bribes and kickbacks that honeycombed New York City government; a company that knowingly marketed an unsafe birth control device; the decision-making process that led to the space shuttle Challenger tragedy.

"When in doubt, don't."

The stories are always slightly different; but they have a lot in common since they're full of the oldest questions in the world, questions of human behavior and human judgment applied in ordinary day-to-day situations. Reading them we have to ask how usually honest, intelligent, compassionate human beings could act in ways that are callous, dishonest, and wrongheaded.

In my view, the explanations go back to four rationalizations that people have relied on through

Mr. Gellerman is dean of the University of Dallas Graduate School of Management. He is the author of eight books on management and of the HBR article "Supervision: Substance and Style" (March-April 1976).

the ages to justify questionable conduct: believing that the activity is not "really" illegal or immoral; that it is in the individual's or the corporation's best interest; that it will never be found out; or that because it helps the company the company will condone it. By looking at these rationalizations in light of these cases, we can develop some practical rules to more effectively control managers' actions that lead to trouble – control, but not eliminate. For the hard truth is that corporate misconduct, like the lowly cockroach, is a plague that we can suppress but never exterminate.

Three cases

Amitai Etzioni, professor of sociology at George Washington University, recently concluded that in the last ten years, roughly two-thirds of America's 500 largest corporations have been involved, in varying degrees, in some form of illegal behavior. By taking a look at three corporate cases, we may be able to identify the roots of the kind of misconduct that not only ruins some people's lives, destroys institutions, and gives business as a whole a bad name but that also inflicts real and lasting harm on a large number of innocent people. The three cases that follow should be familiar. I present them here as examples of the types of problems that confront managers in all kinds of businesses daily.

Manville Corporation

A few years ago, Manville (then Johns Manville) was solid enough to be included among the giants of American business. Today Manville is in the process of turning over 80% of its equity to a trust representing people who have sued or plan to sue it for liability in connection with one of its principal former products, asbestos. For all practical purposes, the entire company was brought down by questions of corporate ethics.

More than 40 years ago, information began to reach Johns Manville's medical department—and through it, the company's top executives—implicating asbestos inhalation as a cause of asbestosis, a debilitating lung disease, as well as lung cancer and mesothelioma, an invariably fatal lung disease. Manville's managers suppressed the research. Moreover, as a matter of policy, they apparently decided to conceal the information from affected employees. The company's medical staff collaborated in the cover-up, for reasons we can only guess at.

Money may have been one motive. In one particularly chilling piece of testimony, a lawyer recalled how 40 years earlier he had confronted Manville's corporate counsel about the company's policy of concealing chest X-ray results from employees. The lawyer had asked, "Do you mean to tell me you would let them work until they dropped dead?" The reply was, "Yes, we save a lot of money that way."

Based on such testimony, a California court found that Manville had hidden the asbestos danger from its employees rather than looking for safer ways to handle it. It was less expensive to pay workers' compensation claims than to develop safer working conditions. A New Jersey court was even blunter: it found that Manville had made a conscious, cold-blooded business decision to take no protective or remedial action, in flagrant disregard of the rights of others.

How can we explain this behavior? Were more than 40 years' worth of Manville executives all immoral?

Such an answer defies common sense. The truth, I think, is less glamorous—and also less satisfying to those who like to explain evil as the actions of a few misbegotten souls. The people involved were probably ordinary men and women for the most part, not very different from you and me. They found themselves in a dilemma, and they solved it in a way that seemed to be the least troublesome, deciding not to disclose information that could hurt their product. The consequences of what they chose to do—both to thousands of innocent people and, ultimately, to the corporation—probably never occurred to them.

The Manville case illustrates the fine line between acceptable and unacceptable managerial behavior. Executives are expected to strike a difficult balance—to pursue their companies' best interests but not overstep the bounds of what outsiders will tolerate.

Even the best managers can find themselves in a bind, not knowing how far is too far. In retrospect, they can usually easily tell where they should have drawn the line, but no one manages in retrospect. We can only live and act today and hope that whoever looks back on what we did will judge that we struck the proper balance. In a few years, many of us may be found delinquent for decisions we are making now about tobacco, clean air, the use of chemicals, or some other seemingly benign substance. The managers at Manville may have believed that they were acting in the company's best interests, or that what they were doing would never be found out, or even that it wasn't really wrong. In the end, these were only rationalizations for conduct that brought the company down.

Continental Illinois Bank

Until recently the ninth largest bank in the United States, Continental Illinois had to be saved from insolvency because of bad judgment by management. The government bailed it out, but at a price. In effect it has been socialized: about 80% of its equity now belongs to the Federal Deposit Insurance Corporation. Continental seems to have been brought down by managers who misunderstood its real interests. To their own peril, executives focused on a single-minded pursuit of corporate ends and forgot about the means to the ends.

In 1976, Continental's chairman declared that within five years the magnitude of its lending would match that of any other bank. The goal was attainable; in fact, for a time, Continental reached it. But it dictated a shift in strategy away from conservative corporate financing and toward aggressive pursuit of borrowers. So Continental, with lots of lendable funds, sent its loan officers into the field to buy loans that had originally been made by smaller banks that had less money.

The practice in itself was not necessarily unsound. But some of the smaller banks had done more than just lend money—they had swallowed hook, line, and sinker the extravagant, implausible dreams of poorly capitalized oil producers in Oklahoma, and they had begun to bet enormous sums on those dreams. Eventually, a cool billion dollars' worth of those dreams found their way into Continental's portfolio, and a cool billion dollars of depositors' money flowed out to pay for them. When the price of oil fell, a lot of dry holes and idle drilling equipment were all that was left to show for most of the money.

Continental's officers had become so entranced by their lending efforts' spectacular results that they hadn't looked deeply into how they had been achieved. Huge sums of money were lent at fat rates of interest. If the borrowers had been able to repay the loans, Continental might have become the eighth or even the seventh largest bank in the country. But that was a very big "if." Somehow there was a failure of control and judgment at Continental—probably because the officers who were buying those shaky loans

"...So that's how the destabilization is going down here. How's the deregulation going up there?"

were getting support and praise from their superiors. Or at least they were not hearing enough tough questions about them.

At one point, for example, Continental's internal auditors stumbled across the fact that an officer who had purchased $800 million in oil and gas loans from the Penn Square Bank in Oklahoma City had also borrowed $565,000 for himself from Penn Square. Continental's top management investigated and eventually issued a reprimand. The mild rebuke reflected the officer's hard work and the fact that the portfolio he had obtained would have yielded an average return of nearly 20% had it ever performed as planned. In fact, virtually all of the $800 million had to be written off. Management chose to interpret the incident charitably; federal prosecutors later alleged a kickback.

On at least two other occasions, Continental's own control mechanisms flashed signals that something was seriously wrong with the oil and gas

portfolio. A vice president warned in a memo that the documentation needed to verify the soundness of many of the purchased loans had simply never arrived. Later, a junior loan officer, putting his job on the line, went over the heads of three superiors to tell a top executive about the missing documentation. Management chose not to investigate. After all, Continental was doing exactly what its chairman had said it would do: it was on its way to becoming the leading commercial lender in the United States. Oil and gas loans were an important factor in that achievement. Stopping to wait for paperwork to catch up would only slow down reaching the goal.

Eventually, however, the word got out about the instability of the bank's portfolio, which led to a massive run on its deposits. No other bank was willing to come to the rescue, for fear of being swamped by Continental's huge liabilities. To avoid going under, Continental in effect became a ward of the federal government. The losers were the bank's shareholders, some officers who lost their jobs, at least one who was indicted, and some 2,000 employees (about 15% of the total) who were let go, as the bank scaled down to fit its diminished assets.

Once again, it is easy for us to sit in judgment after the fact and say that Continental's loan officers and their superiors were doing exactly what bankers shouldn't do: they were gambling with their depositors' money. But on another level, this story is more difficult to analyze – and more generally a part of everyday business. Certainly part of Continental's problem was neglect of standard controls. But another dimension involved ambitious corporate goals. Pushed by lofty goals, managers could not see clearly their real interests. They focused on ends, overlooked the ethical questions associated with their choice of means – and ultimately hurt themselves.

E.F. Hutton

The nation's second largest independent broker, E.F. Hutton & Company, recently pleaded guilty to 2,000 counts of mail and wire fraud. It had systematically bilked 400 of its banks by drawing against uncollected funds or in some cases against nonexistent sums, which it then covered after having enjoyed interest-free use of the money. So far, Hutton has agreed to pay a fine of $2 million as well as the government's investigation costs of $750,000. It has set up an $8 million reserve for restitution to the banks – which may not be enough. Several officers have lost their jobs, and some indictments may yet follow.

But worst of all, Hutton has tarnished its reputation, never a wise thing to do – certainly not when your business is offering to handle other people's money. Months after Hutton agreed to appoint new directors—as a way to give outsiders a solid majority on the board—the company couldn't find people to accept the seats, in part because of the bad publicity.

Apparently Hutton's branch managers had been encouraged to pay close attention to cash management. At some point, it dawned on someone that using other people's money was even more profitable than using your own. In each case, Hutton's overdrafts involved no large sums. But cumulatively, the savings on interest that would otherwise have been owed to the banks was very large. Because Hutton always made covering deposits, and because most banks did not object, Hutton assured its managers that what they were doing was sharp—and not shady. They presumably thought they were pushing legality to its limit without going over the line. The branch managers were simply taking full advantage of what the law and the bankers' tolerance permitted. On several occasions, the managers who played this game most astutely were even congratulated for their skill.

Hutton probably will not suffer a fate as drastic as Manville's or Continental Illinois's. Indeed, with astute damage control, it can probably emerge from this particular embarrassment with only a few bad memories. But this case has real value because it is typical of much corporate misconduct. Most improprieties don't cut a corporation off at the knees the way Manville's and Continental Illinois's did. In fact, most such actions are never revealed at all—or at least that's how people figure things will work out. And in many cases, a willingness to gamble thus is probably enhanced by the rationalization—true or not—that everyone else is doing something just as bad or would if they could; that those who wouldn't go for their share are idealistic fools.

Four rationalizations

Why do managers do things that ultimately inflict great harm on their companies, themselves, and people on whose patronage or tolerance their organizations depend? These three cases, as well as the current crop of examples in each day's paper, supply ample evidence of the motivations and instincts that underlie corporate misconduct. Although the particulars may vary—from the gruesome dishonesty surrounding asbestos handling to the mundanity of illegal money management—the motivating beliefs are pretty much the same. We may examine them in the context of the corporation, but we know that these feelings are basic throughout society; we find them wherever we go because we take them with us.

When we look more closely at these cases, we can delineate four commonly held rationalizations that can lead to misconduct:

A belief that the activity is within reasonable ethical and legal limits—that is, that it is not "really" illegal or immoral.

A belief that the activity is in the individual's or the corporation's best interests—that the individual would somehow be expected to undertake the activity.

A belief that the activity is "safe" because it will never be found out or publicized; the classic crime-and-punishment issue of discovery.

A belief that because the activity helps the company the company will condone it and even protect the person who engages in it.

☐ The idea that an action is not really wrong is an old issue. How far is too far? Exactly where is the line between smart and too smart? Between sharp and shady? Between profit maximization and illegal conduct? The issue is complex: it involves an interplay between top management's goals and middle managers' efforts to interpret those aims.

Put enough people in an ambiguous, ill-defined situation, and some will conclude that whatever hasn't been labeled specifically wrong must be OK—especially if they are rewarded for certain acts. Deliberate overdrafts, for example, were not proscribed at Hutton. Since the company had not spelled out their illegality, it could later plead guilty for itself while shielding its employees from prosecution.

Top executives seldom ask their subordinates to do things that both of them know are against the law or imprudent. But company leaders sometimes leave things unsaid or give the impression that there are things they don't want to know about. In other words, they can seem, whether deliberately or otherwise, to be distancing themselves from their subordinates' tactical decisions in order to keep their own hands clean if things go awry. Often they lure ambitious lower level managers by implying that rich rewards await those who can produce certain results—and that the methods for achieving them will not be examined too closely. Continental's simple wrist-slapping of the officer who was caught in a flagrant conflict of interest sent a clear message to other managers about what top management really thought was important.

How can managers avoid crossing a line that is seldom precise? Unfortunately, most know that they have overstepped it only when they have gone too far. They have no reliable guidelines about what will be overlooked or tolerated or what will be condemned or attacked. When managers must operate in murky borderlands, their most reliable guideline is an old principle: when in doubt, don't.

That may seem like a timid way to run a business. One could argue that if it actually took hold among the middle managers who run most companies, it might take the enterprise out of free enterprise. But there is a difference between taking a worthwhile economic risk and risking an illegal act to make more money.

The difference between becoming a success and becoming a statistic lies in knowledge – including self-knowledge – not daring. Contrary to popular mythology, managers are not paid to take risks; they are paid to know which risks are worth taking. Also, maximizing profits is a company's second priority, not its first. The first is ensuring its survival.

All managers risk giving too much because of what their companies demand from them. But the same superiors who keep pressing you to do more, or to do it better, or faster, or less expensively, will turn on you should you cross that fuzzy line between right and wrong. They will blame you for exceeding instructions or for ignoring their warnings. The smartest managers already know that the best answer to the question, "How far is too far?" is don't try to find out.

☐   Turning to the second reason why people take risks that get their companies into trouble, believing that unethical conduct is in a person's or corporation's best interests nearly always results from a parochial view of what those interests are. For example, Alpha Industries, a Massachusetts manufacturer of microwave equipment, paid $57,000 to a Raytheon manager, ostensibly for a marketing report. Air force investigators charged that the report was a ruse to cover a bribe: Alpha wanted subcontracts that the Raytheon manager supervised. But those contracts ultimately cost Alpha a lot more than they paid for the report. After the company was indicted for bribery, its contracts were suspended and its profits promptly vanished. Alpha wasn't unique in this transgression: in 1984, the Pentagon suspended 453 other companies for violating procurement regulations.

Ambitious managers look for ways to attract favorable attention, something to distinguish them from other people. So they try to outperform their peers. Some may see that it is not difficult to look remarkably good in the short run by avoiding things that pay off only in the long run. For example, you can skimp on maintenance or training or customer service, and you can get away with it – for a while.

The sad truth is that many managers have been promoted on the basis of "great" results obtained in just those ways, leaving unfortunate successors to inherit the inevitable whirlwind. Since this is not necessarily a just world, the problems that such people create are not always traced back to them. Companies cannot afford to be hoodwinked in this way. They must be concerned with more than just results. They have to look very hard at how results are obtained.

Evidently, in Hutton's case there were such reviews, but management chose to interpret favorably what government investigators later interpreted unfavorably. This brings up another dilemma: management quite naturally hopes that any of its borderline actions will be overlooked or at least interpreted charitably if noticed. Companies must accept human nature for what it is and protect themselves with watchdogs to sniff out possible misdeeds.

An independent auditing agency that reports to outside directors can play such a role. It can provide a less comfortable, but more convincing, review of how management's successes are achieved. The discomfort can be considered inexpensive insurance and serve to remind all employees that the real interests of the company are served by honest conduct in the first place.

☐   The third reason why a risk is taken, believing that one can probably get away with it, is perhaps the most difficult to deal with because it's often true. A great deal of proscribed behavior escapes detection.

We know that conscience alone does not deter everyone. For example, First National Bank of Boston pleaded guilty to laundering satchels of $20 bills worth $1.3 billion. Thousands of satchels must have passed through the bank's doors without incident before the scheme was detected. That kind of heavy, unnoticed traffic breeds complacency.

How can we deter wrongdoing that is unlikely to be detected? Make it more likely to be detected. Had today's "discovery" process – in which plaintiff's attorneys can comb through a company's records to look for incriminating evidence – been in use when Manville concealed the evidence on asbestosis, there probably would have been no cover-up. Mindful of the likelihood of detection, Manville would have chosen a different course and could very well be thriving today without the protection of the bankruptcy courts.

The most effective deterrent is not to increase the severity of punishment for those caught but to heighten the perceived probability of being caught in the first place. For example, police have found that parking an empty patrol car at locations where motorists often exceed the speed limit reduces the frequency of speeding. Neighborhood "crime watch" signs that people display decrease burglaries.

Simply increasing the frequency of audits and spot checks is a deterrent, especially when combined with three other simple techniques: scheduling audits irregularly, making at least half of them unannounced, and setting up some checkups soon after others. But frequent spot checks cost more than big sticks, a fact that raises the question of which approach is more cost-effective.

A common managerial error is to assume that because frequent audits uncover little behavior that is out of line, less frequent, and therefore less costly, auditing is sufficient. But this condition overlooks the important deterrent effect of frequent checking. The point is to prevent misconduct, not just to catch it.

A trespass detected should not be dealt with discreetly. Managers should announce the misconduct and how the individuals involved were punished. Since the main deterrent to illegal or unethical behavior is the perceived probability of detection, managers should make an example of people who are detected.

☐   Let's look at the fourth reason why corporate misconduct tends to occur, a belief that the company will condone actions that are taken in its interest and will even protect the managers responsible. The question we have to deal with here is, How do we keep company loyalty from going berserk?

That seems to be what happened at Manville. A small group of executives and a succession of corporate medical directors kept the facts about the lethal qualities of asbestos from becoming public knowledge for decades, and they managed to live with that knowledge. And at Manville, the company—or really, the company's senior management—did condone their decision and protect those employees.

Something similar seems to have happened at General Electric. When one of its missile projects ran up costs greater than the air force had agreed to pay, middle managers surreptitiously shifted those costs to projects that were still operating under budget. In this case, the loyalty that ran amok was primarily to the division: managers want their units' results to look good. But GE, with one of the finest reputations in U.S. industry, was splattered with scandal and paid a fine of $1.04 million.

One of the most troubling aspects of the GE case is the company's admission that those involved were thoroughly familiar with the company's ethical standards before the incident took place. This suggests that the practice of declaring codes of ethics and teaching them to managers is not enough to deter unethical conduct. Something stronger is needed.

Top management has a responsibility to exert a moral force within the company. Senior executives are responsible for drawing the line between loyalty to the company and action against the laws and values of the society in which the company must operate. Further, because that line can be obscured in the heat of the moment, the line has to be drawn well short of where reasonable men and women could begin to suspect that their rights had been violated. The company has to react long before a prosecutor, for instance, would have a strong enough case to seek an indictment.

Executives have a right to expect loyalty from employees against competitors and detractors, but not loyalty against the law, or against common morality, or against society itself. Managers must warn employees that a disservice to customers, and especially to innocent bystanders, cannot be a service to the company. Finally, and most important of all, managers must stress that excuses of company loyalty will not be accepted for acts that place its good name in jeopardy. To put it bluntly, superiors must make it clear that employees who harm other people allegedly for the company's benefit will be fired.

The most extreme examples of corporate misconduct were due, in hindsight, to managerial failures. A good way to avoid management oversights is to subject the control mechanisms themselves to periodic surprise audits, perhaps as a function of the board of directors. The point is to make sure that internal audits and controls are functioning as planned. It's a case of inspecting the inspectors and taking the necessary steps to keep the controls working efficiently. Harold Geneen, former head of ITT, has suggested that the board should have an independent staff, something analogous to the Government Accounting Office, which reports to the legislative rather than the executive branch. In the end, it is up to top management to send a clear and pragmatic message to all employees that good ethics is still the foundation of good business. ▽

Reprint 86402

Why history matters to managers

*A roundtable discussion
on the value
of having managers
study history and
a graduate school of business
administration teach it*

*Participants:
Alfred D. Chandler, Jr.,
Thomas K. McCraw,
Alonzo L. McDonald
Richard S. Tedlow, and
Richard H.K. Vietor*

*Edited by
Alan M. Kantrow*

At a time when many of the long-established practices and assumptions of American managers have fallen under serious challenge, practitioners and professors alike have needed to take a hard look at how they understand the challenges and responsibilities of management.

To what extent has practice become riddled by the curse of easy formulas? How far has the temptation of the quick fix distorted complex choices? In what fashion has the impulse to view future conditions as a simple extrapolation of present trends played havoc with today's decisions? A changed competitive world has made answering these, and many other such questions, a matter of no small urgency.

On this task, the study and teaching of history have helped shed much light. If the quality of executives' judgment is to improve and if executives are to be able to draw with confidence and intelligence on the experience of others, they must first know how to read the lessons embedded in that experience. Here, as the discussants show in a variety of ways, lies the value of history in management—and in management education.

Mr. Chandler is Isidor Straus Professor of Business History at the Harvard Business School and editor of Harvard Studies in Business History. *He is the author of* Strategy & Structure: Chapters in the History of the American Industrial Enterprise *(MIT Press, 1962) and of the*

Pulitzer Prize-winning The Visible Hand: The Managerial Revolution in American Business *(Harvard University Press, 1977).*

Mr. McCraw is a professor of general management at HBS where he teaches a course on business, government, and the international economy. He is also author of two books on the TVA as well as of the Pulitzer Prize-winning Prophets of Regulation *(Harvard University Press, 1984).*

Mr. McDonald is chairman of the board and CEO of Avenir Group. He was previously president and vice chairman of Bendix Corporation, managing director of McKinsey & Company, and special assistant to the president of the United States. Once a member of the faculty at HBS, he now acts as counsel to the dean.

Mr. Tedlow, an assistant professor at HBS in marketing and editor of the Business History Review, *is author of* Keeping the Corporate Image: Public Relations and Business, 1900-1950 *(JAI Press, 1980). He is also co-author, with Alfred Chandler, of* The Coming of Managerial Capitalism: A Casebook on the History of American Economic Institutions *(Richard D. Irwin, 1985).*

Mr. Vietor is a professor of general management at HBS, where he teaches a course on regulation, and is also author of Energy Policy in America Since 1945 *(Cambridge University Press, 1984).*

Photomontage by Karen Watson.

Chandler: Don't forget, the heart of this school's curriculum has always been the case study, and the case study is precisely what a historian does, what a historian is trained to do.

McDonald: Let me talk a bit from my point of view as a consultant. One of the first things you do when looking at a major problem is to try to define the context or environment in which to place that problem. Only then does the problem really begin to take on meaning, make its true severity clear, or point the way toward management actions that might resolve it.

Tedlow: If you think about it, what Al Chandler has been able to do—in his own writing and in his development of the business history course here—is set up a context within which historians can effectively examine business enterprise and ask questions of it that are interesting and useful. He's provided the context.

You know, when you're teaching here, there's no feeling in the gut that's worse than when you feel you have lost the thread of the course, that somehow you are just teaching a string of cases and nothing more. Many times, it is history that supplies that thread and helps to give order to a mass of experience.

McDonald: There's something else, too, beyond this issue of perspective. It is always hard to communicate any sort of abstract idea to someone else, let alone get any acceptance of it. But when there is some agreement on the factual or historical background of that idea, the possibilities for general agreement expand enormously. In other words, the kind of historical work we have been talking about can help provide semantic abbreviations that, in turn, facilitate communication.

Tedlow: I couldn't agree more. One of the most important functions of business history is to make sure that the analogies we use in thinking about things are correct.

McCraw: Look, we all agree that history is a way of thinking—a way of searching for patterns and trying to see if such patterns recur from one situation to another. It helps us think about the parameters of what's possible, what the boundaries of likely action or possible success are. It is a search for pattern.

Tedlow: Let's not forget another, equally important use of history—that is, simply getting things, events, and facts into shared memory. Let me give you a specific example. When we talk about labor and government in our courses here, it is important for our students to know something about, say, the [General Motors] Flint Strike in Michigan in 1936-1937. Why? Well, when our students get into management and have to deal with workers and unions, the people across the table will have heard about that strike. For many years, UAW journals and magazines commemorated it and carried accounts of the celebrations and speeches with which the unions have kept the memory of that strike alive. It is terribly important for our students to know this kind of stuff because they are going to have to deal with the heritage of disrespect that has grown up between unions and management.

McDonald: Let me expand on that point a bit. It seems to me that history in business is not useful just as a kind of academic or intellectual exercise. It has to do with an established set of facts—in the same way that a financial exhibit has to do with an established set of numbers—which one then has to interpret. An underlying concept or vision is fundamental to all the major decisions that get made at the top of a corporation. One of the most important things a CEO can say is, "This is our philosophy, this is the general direction in which we are going, this is the perspective from which we need to view the issues before us at the moment." Having a historical concept supplies a solid reference point.

In fact, when I was overseas, we used to have a saying that in McKinsey's practice we could export ways of thinking about a problem but we could not export solutions. In each case we had to go back to the thought process itself in order to come up with the appropriate solutions because each case took place in a different historical and cultural context, in a different environment.

Now, if you don't have this kind of idea or historical perspective, there is an enormous temptation to make a managerial mistake that could be financially traumatic—and to make it simply by using aspiration instead of reality in the decision framework. You just don't want to be in the position of going to your board and saying the situation you face is unique, has never confronted human beings before, and demands a course of action no one has ever tried. True, no two sets of circumstances are ever entirely identical, but often there is a general pattern which does repeat from setting to setting.

Chandler: This goes back, of course, to one of the oldest problems of all: reinventing the wheel. Much of this goes on. Just think of the problems that exist between marketers and production people and of the people who talk about those problems as if they were something new. Well, they're not.

McDonald: I want to interject a discordant note here. One of the things we need to be cau-

From left to right
Thomas K. McCraw, Alonzo L. McDonald, Richard S. Tedlow,
Alfred D. Chandler, Jr., Richard H.K. Vietor

tious about is not undercutting the ability of our students to perceive points of discontinuity. I may not, for example, live long enough in my current executive position to experience the long-term continuity you all tell me might be there. Day to day, what I have to cope with are the ripples on the surface that appear to me to be entirely discontinuous.

Even though I need the reassurance of pattern, it would be a bad mistake for me to look only at the fact of pattern. Just because a certain kind of business cycle has always bounced back in the past does not mean that it will bounce back the next time. Believing that it will can be fatal in certain businesses – especially today, with the changes in pace, complexity, and the number of variables that managers confront.

McCraw: Mark Twain once said that history doesn't repeat itself but sometimes it rhymes. That's about the best it does and sometimes it does not even do that.

Chandler: That's right. The other side of the coin is to be able to recognize that some things really are different from anything that came before. In the 1850s, for example, when railroads became important, you simply could not run a railroad the way you managed anything that came before. Anybody that tried to do it that way quickly found that the effort wasn't worth it.

McCraw: Look, at base, all of us here are comparativists as well as historians, and so we believe that the way that you find out whether you are in a continuum or in the midst of a discontinuity is to triangulate your position the way a navigator does with the stars. In this business of finding out where you are, we believe that you constantly have to compare where you are with where you've been, with where the other democratic market economies are, and so on.

This emphasis on the comparative method really helps in the process of sorting out whether a given set of events represents a discontinuity. It also helps define the relationship between what a manager can do in a given situation and what the general historical forces operating at the time are forcing everyone to do, no matter what the individual's preference. This is one of the issues that Dick [Vietor] tries to address in his course on regulation–namely, just what is the value added that an individual manager can bring in the midst of broad, sweeping historical changes.

Vietor: True enough, but even if the changes are discontinuous, you can look to history to help figure out what's going on. As Tom suggests, in my course on regulation I try to arrange at least six or eight classes in a kind of module, each of which traces the evolution of regulation in a single industry or business sector.

Take the deregulation of the telecommunications industry, for example. You want to understand how the regulations originally affected the segmentation of the market, how they changed the market, and what reversing those regulations or removing them will do. The historical context helps you see what challenges are being presented now.

Chandler: The hardest thing in all of this is to help our students appreciate the sheer complexity of the real world.

Tedlow: One of the things we try to combat is the students' real desire for formulas–a wish for a fact or interpretation that must be *the* key, *the* answer. They're a little uncomfortable with the great boom and buzzing confusion of how complex things are, and it has always struck me that one of the most valuable things you can learn from history is what you cannot learn from history. It's good to be reminded that there are no keys, no formulas. Just look at the number of people who drew perfectly reasonable conclusions from what had happened in the past but were terribly wrong.

Vietor: Sure, think of the electric utility capacity planners in 1972 when they negotiated for the construction of six nuclear power plants because they saw a trend line out 30 years or so of 7.1% annual growth in demand.

McDonald: These folks were wrong because they were accepting a solution pattern rather than rethinking the problem. The kind of history we are talking about is not a handy set of solutions but a thought process, a thought process by which the variables that will influence some result can be identified or stroked to some degree, and people can make an attempt to understand them and their implications.

McCraw: Let me say that differently. History offers another way of thinking that helps teach people to accept ambiguity, to be comfortable with it, and to reject formulas.

Tedlow: Yes, I think that being comfortable with ambiguity is, perhaps, one of the most important uses of history. It helps prevent people from acting on invalid historical analogies.

Vietor: I think that may have been AT&T's problem during the 1970s.

Tedlow: Let me go back to the basic question of whether a given change is part of a real discontinuity or merely part of something cyclical. I have never seen a better discussion of that than the Du Pont chapter in *Strategy & Structure*. Remember, they developed a strategy to go into the paint business because they thought it was just like the dynamite business. There were no barriers to entry; there was only one other big company. They thought they would be able to win there with scale. The thing is, they kept on losing money, and the more paint they made, the more money they lost.

So they did a study with internal consultants–a group of folks, some of whom were quite young. The question they found themselves wrestling with was, "Is this a big problem or is it not?" And they said, "Ah, it is a big problem and what we need is a basic structural change." This answer went back up to the top of the company, and one of the people at the top said, "No, we are losing money because we are new to the business. We are not managing inventory right; we're just not doing business right. It is the same kind of problem we have had before." It took shock treatment, specifically in the form of miserable earnings reports, to get management to believe that it really was a big problem.

McDonald: No matter what you do, people are going to leave school with a pet formula or two that they really think will help them know all the answers. From a professional manager's point of view, one of our chief tasks is to knock that thought out of them their first year at work or at least during their first five years. Some of them soon learn a touch of humility; others don't. The ones who do, prosper. Those who don't have a pretty hard time.

You know, when I came back to teaching, it had been 25 years or so since I had left the Business School, and during the time I was away I did not have much contact with the student body. One of the first things that struck me when I got back was the high degree of personal control that students believe they have over their destinies and the destinies of their enterprises. That contrasts, of course, with the more humble degrees of expectation about control that they have in the later stages of their careers. Early on, they will point to something that did not go well and say, "Well, it's his fault, or her fault, or why did that person do that?" It is easy to think that some situation represents the pinnacle of absolute stupidity until you become a victim of circumstance yourself.

It's also the case, though, that the historical context becomes even more important later on in your career than it is in the beginning. As managers begin to be aware of the restraints or pressures within which they have to operate—and these are very real barriers—they come to have some increased appreciation of all the forces that can affect what they can actually do.

Now, I'm sure that if you asked older managers whether they thought a lot about historical context, they would say no. But if you asked them about the first issue they raise when meeting with the CEO of a company they plan to acquire, they would say, "Well, I want to know about the company, about how you got to be where you are, about how things got to be the way they are." Of course, these are *historical* questions.

McCraw: It's just that more history has happened to experienced people.

Vietor: I've done some teaching of historical materials to middle managers in telecommunications. In some instances, senior managers have perspective on the changes that are taking place, but for the most part middle managers do not because they have been in the trenches and have seen only a very small piece of what's going on. So I often get quite a pleased reaction from them that, for the first time, they can see where they fit in the larger scheme of things and can understand which way things are going, the direction of movement. I'm not sure that all this leads them to any sort of concrete action, position, or blueprint, but the feeling that things fit into a larger context helps them. It gives them a sense of perspective that they did not have before.

Chandler: Yes, but it is important to do more than just drown them in facts about the past. You need to show them how one period was different from another—as the 1850s were different from the 1840s—because if there is no such attempt to structure one thing against the other, you can get lost so very quickly. But when you do structure things right, as time passes, students will begin to get a feel for the complexity of things.

McCraw: That's right. One of the reasons that those of us who are professional historians have found a home here at the Harvard Business School has to do with the nature of the curriculum and with the way we teach. In the first place, the empirical orientation of most historians matches up almost perfectly with this school's insistence on facts and with its determination to study the world as it actually is. In this,

we are distinct from several of the other major business schools, which tend to rely more on mathematical models of the way the world might be. We also feel so comfortable here because what we do—and what the school does—is to study change. That is, we are concerned with identifying change, with identifying the reasons that things happen as they do, and with the balance between inevitability and managerial choice.

Tedlow: Let me give you an example from a recent seminar discussion on the Japanese steel industry. It turns out that the Japanese steel manufacturers came to rely on the basic oxygen furnace while the steel companies in the United States continued to rely on the open-hearth furnace. Lately the U.S. steel makers have been catching it from all sides. Everybody has been telling them all the things that they have done wrong. Well, it's not so simple. There were perfectly good reasons why, at the time, the American steel companies did not adopt the basic oxygen furnace.

It was a process about which they were completely aware, and in fact it was a process that they, at the urging of the U.S. government, introduced to the Japanese. Apparently, they brought the Japanese to Switzerland and Austria and said, "Look at this, this is what you have got to get involved in. We want you to get involved because, if you don't, we are all going to keep bidding up the price of scrap." On the basis of the realities that the American steel producers faced at the time, they made what seemed to be a reasonable decision. It turned out, of course, that they were wrong and that the price of being wrong was terribly high.

McDonald: Like so many others, that decision was costly and also hard to undo. History teaches us that it is often very hard to retreat from Moscow once the snow starts to fall. You know, if you are a salesman in Rapid City and the weather forecast says that there is a storm coming in from the plains, you immediately race for the airport if you do not want to waste another three days.

Decisions have consequences, but that does not make it fair for us to judge those who make them harshly through the benefit of hindsight. Who is to say that they were wrong at the time they made their decision? We make decisions like that every day. Let me tell you, we all hope that if circumstances turn out to be unfavorable, they will not show up that way until well after our retirement.

McCraw: What you are talking about, Al, is the classic historical problem of inevitability. I remember a line—I think it's from James Gould Cozzens—to the effect that, if you look back over the last ten years of your life, everything that happened seems to have been inevitable. It seems that it had to happen that way. You come to accept it and become philosophical about it, and experience a feeling of something like wisdom. But then you look forward ten years and nothing looks inevitable at all. You confront, rather directly, one of the great values of the historical way of thinking: the constant need to find a balance between volition and determinism.

McDonald: You remind me of the old proverb that says, "No matter what path you might choose in order to avoid your fate, you will meet it along the path you choose." That's the inevitable situation managers face as they go about taking on a risk. But there's another point I would like to make here. I've just been reading a report that says, as we have gotten more scientific and sophisticated in our use of computers for decision making, our margin of error has gotten larger and larger. To me this indicates our greater reliance on the process of extrapolation from given facts than on our exercise of judgment about underlying assumptions.

In a small, private investment firm in which I am interested, for example, we have a 13-page analytical format that we've been following when we look at an acquisition. Only the last four pages deal with conclusions – things like expected balance sheets, P&L statements, cash flow, and the ratios. The first nine pages spell out the underlying assumptions in detail because the answers on the last pages all look so very precise, so real. It's easy to treat them that way – it's what the philosopher Whitehead called the "fallacy of misplaced concreteness."

McCraw: We also have to temper our thinking with the knowledge that, by the time we take 5 or 10 years to finish a research project or a book, there will have been 10 or 12 other cycles of pressing issues with which everyone is concerned. Over a year ago I was commissioned to write a paper for a conference on industrial policy. By the time the conference actually took place, the upturn of the business cycle had mooted the whole thing.

Chandler: But think about the other side of the equation too. One of the major advantages for historians at a school like this is that we continually get taught new ways of looking at our material. The shifting questions that our colleagues ask help us ask new things about the historical periods with which we are most familiar. When new industries emerge, new structures get built and whole new ways of competition lock into place. I keep looking back to the 1880s and 1890s as a critical period. Being in this kind of setting at HBS has helped shape my awareness of what was going on back then.

McCraw: The point here, I think, is that being a historian in this context helps us frame our research questions and cut down the wasted motion; it helps keep the wheels from spinning and keeps us from getting involved with trivial research topics.

McDonald: You remind me of the story about the city fellow who drives up to a Maine farmer and asks him how far it is this way to the next town. The farmer says 50 miles. After a while the guy comes back and says that someone else told him that if he made a left turn up ahead, it would only be 3 miles. The guy says, "Why didn't *you* tell me that?" And the farmer replies, "You didn't ask."

McCraw: That's like the old Arkansas joke about the traveler who asks a farmer how to get to Little Rock. The farmer says, "I don't know," and the traveler says, "Well, you're pretty dumb, aren't you?" The farmer replies, "Maybe so, but I'm not the one who is lost."

Vietor: There's another point here worth making. In the last decade or so, the rate of change in the business environment has gotten so fast that simply understanding the context of what has gone on before becomes that much more important if you're going to have any kind of real help in knowing where you're going. When everything is stable and calm and the sea is flat, you can fairly easily go along without paying all that much attention to the kind of history we are talking about. But when everything is in chaos, that's when you need to know about the history of regulation or energy or whatever.

Chandler: But don't forget that at any point you want to pick in the history of this school, your students and colleagues would have said that everything was going along fine up to just about five years ago. The experience of chaos is relative.

McCraw: Not long ago, I wrote an article for the TVA's fiftieth anniversary. The TVA, you know, is in big trouble today as are many utilities because they have all these nuclear plants under construction and have to accept the possibility of huge write-offs. But they've also got an image of a glorious past. Well, I've written two books on the TVA in the 1930s and so I was asked to write a retrospective commentary about those glory days. They expected that I would tell all about the golden years. I didn't give it that title, however. When the piece came out in the employees' magazine, it had a headline that said, "Alleged Golden Years Not True."

From where we stand, it's easy to see why things might appear golden back then, but in fact in the 1930s those guys were going out of their minds. Litigation was everywhere. They didn't know where their paychecks were coming from. Everyone who worked for that organization and made $75 a month or more had to be listed in the annual report as a way of insuring against featherbedding.

Tedlow: At heart, what all historians are really trying to find out is what was really going on, what really happened. That's the first responsibility— that and establishing an accurate ordering of facts.

Vietor: That's right. It's not just establishing the facts but linking them together. If you can take three facts and join them together then you've learned something, learned a lesson about those facts.

Tedlow: And those are the lessons you need when you want to ask basic questions like, "How do you manage when you're number one? How do you know when and how to change when you're the leader?"

At the turn of the century, three of the leading companies in Chicago were Swift, Pullman, and International Harvester. What happened? In 1920, Ford was the leading car company in the world. Every other car was a Model T. What happened? Studying history helps give you some idea of the domain over which managers actually do have power and influence. It helps you see where you can have an effect. It helps you understand what happened—and what *can* happen.

Look, it was not at all inevitable that John D. Rockefeller would become the great entrepreneur of the oil industry. Rockefeller made a lot of individual decisions, day by day, which in total enabled him to become a billionaire at a time when the gross national product of the United States was something like $35 billion. But there were things he could not have done, no matter how hard he tried. He could not have built an oil industry that was structured along the lines of the apparel industry. Nobody could. He was in a huge scale-based industry, and the greatest manager in the world couldn't have made a success out of it by treating it as something else.

Vietor: One of the things we have learned, again and again, is that you can bet on continuity only with a high degree of risk. If you are about to invest in petrochemicals in Japan on the assumption there is going to be a stable supply of crude oil for a long time, you are going to be in trouble rather quickly. If you want to make a major capital investment assuming long-term stability in public policy, you're crazy because public policy is extremely fickle.

Policies change as frequently as markets do. Now, this doesn't mean that you cannot make decisions or define an appropriate course of action. You can, but you ought to think about a course of action that is flexible enough to survive the kinds of change you are likely to face.

Tedlow: This comes back to my question: How do you change before you have to? The genius of John D. Rockefeller was that he changed that company when he owned the market, when he was by far the leader. He made major, fundamental changes a long time before he had to. But he understood what was coming.

Chandler: Or think about Sloan's great achievement at GM. Every time there was a serious problem, he was there. He was there in the early 1920s when the corporate structure needed a massive reshaping. He was there when basic strategy had to be defined. He was there when the dealers were having a rough time at the beginning of the Depression. He was there when labor tensions blew up in the 1930s. He was there when the war created a host of problems. There are always options open to managers, and the truly good ones know how to start with the limits— with what you can and can't do.

McDonald: But the thing about Sloan is not only what he decided to do but also the way in which he went about doing it. He handled things in a manner that kept them from becoming explosive. He contained them. You know, in addition to the changes that are precipitated by external actions that come as a complete shock, there are plenty of changes that people with foresight can plan for and can accommodate. They are predictable.

There are changes that come when an operation moves from a start-up phase, for example, into a growth posture and then into a mature business. There is no need to spin those wheels each time. We know within general limits what is required to manage at each of these stages, to run things appropriately within these levels. When you don't know any history, however, you are always surprised at what is demanded of you at each of these stages. Managers often do absolutely stupid things that they do not have to do and would not have done if they only understood more about the whole historical sequence. Sloan understood these things.

Vietor: That's what we mean when we talk about perspective, the ability to see things as they are and to understand how to triangulate them for meaning. The book I've just written is about the energy industry and government policy. If you don't see that the rise and fall of oil prices set the parameters of the public policy process, then the kinds of developments that take place on the government side make no sense. You just missed the boat. It all seems like a linear progression toward excess government, but that's dead wrong.

The focus of the kind of history we do is on structure—on understanding the connections among external forces, functional necessities, and the structure of organizations. We need to know not just *that* certain things happened but also *why* and *how*.

Tedlow: Just look at what happens when people take the attitude that certain things are inevitable because they have no understanding of why things happen as they do. The president of the American Economic Association told its convention in 1932 that the labor movement did very badly in the 1920s and that there was no reason at all to believe that it was going to do any better in the 1930s. Except, of course, that the movement organized a full quarter of the labor force during that decade.

And then there's a little book that everybody ought to read, which was written back in 1931 or so, with the title *Oh Yeah*. It is just a series of quotations from people in the late 1920s about how great things were and about how they were going to do nothing but continue to get better. Oh yeah?

McDonald: People always have a tendency to extrapolate from past events because we all fear the risk of attempting to forecast from a movable base line. How long ago was it—two years—when everyone thought the price of oil was going to march straight up to $50 a barrel? My strong suspicion is that, when the price of oil turns around as it will in a few years, everybody is going to be just as shocked as they were the last time. In a corporate setting, though, if you know your history, you know what to expect. If you are moving into a recession or if you're going through a very difficult period, you just know what the budgets are going to look like. You know before the figures come in. What we are really talking about here is the quality of judgment.

Vietor: Let's not forget, though, that during the energy crunch historians waited in gas lines just like everybody else.

McCraw: I thought you were going to say that at least they were first in line. ⊽

Reprint 86109

Do we ever know anything new?

To put the matter most simply: A Greek man of letters like Aristophanes, a Greek philosopher like Plato, if miraculously brought to earth in the midtwentieth century and given speech with us (but no knowledge since his death) could talk fairly soon about literature or philosophy with a G.B. Shaw or a John Dewey, and feel quite at home; a Greek scientist like Archimedes in the same position would, even though he were a genius, need to spend a good many days grinding over elementary and advanced textbooks of physics and acquiring enough mathematics before he could begin to talk shop with a modern physicist like Bohr or Einstein. To put it another way: A modern American college student is not wiser than one of the sages of antiquity, has no better taste than an artist of antiquity, but he knows a lot more physics than the greatest Greek scientist ever knew. He knows more *facts* about literature and philosophy than the wisest Greek of 400 B.C. could know; but in physics he not only knows more facts—he understands the relations between facts, that is, the theories and laws....

The foregoing necessarily oversimplifies the distinction between cumulative and noncumulative knowledge. Notably, for generations of Western thinkers, as for many thinkers today, that part of human knowledge not subsumed under "science" is given less than justice by the tag "noncumulative." It can be argued that what are commonly called the social sciences have in their own right, not just as rather feeble imitations of the natural sciences, an accumulated body of knowledge about the interrelations of human beings. This knowledge is an accumulation not merely of facts, but also of valid interpretations of the facts. Thus economists, in the century and a half from Adam Smith to Lord Keynes, have come to *understand* more about economic activity. It can be argued that philosophers, though they still face some of the questions that faced Plato and Aristotle, have over the centuries improved their methods of analysis, and have refined into greater precision the questions they ask themselves. Finally, though the cynic may say that all we learn from history is that we never learn from history, most of us would hold that over the centuries Western men have built up a body of wisdom and good taste that was not available to the Greeks. How widely such wisdom and taste are spread in our society is another question.

From
The Shaping of Modern Thought
by Crane Brinton
(Englewood Cliffs: Prentice-Hall, Inc.)
Copyright © 1950
Reprinted with permission
of the publisher.

Getting Things Done

Peter F. Drucker

How to make people decisions

There is no magic to good staffing and promotion decisions – just hard work and disciplined thought

Why is it that some managers have a golden touch when it comes to putting the right people in the right jobs? Have they mastered some abstruse method of predicting performance? Have they hit on some wondrous algorithm for personnel evaluation? Not at all, argues Peter Drucker, who draws on his long study of how effective managers operate to identify the key rules and assumptions for matching jobs with people. Instead of magic, what successful matching requires is careful understanding of the most important capabilities that a given job requires and of the strengths and weaknesses of each candidate. No mystery here, just good management.

Mr. Drucker is Clarke Professor of Social Sciences and Management at the Claremont Graduate School and professor emeritus of management at the Graduate Business School of New York University. He is the widely respected author of innumerable books and articles, including more than 20 contributions to HBR.

Executives spend more time on managing people and making people decisions than on anything else – and they should. No other decisions are so long lasting in their consequences or so difficult to unmake. And yet, by and large, executives make poor promotion and staffing decisions. By all accounts, their batting average is no better than .333: at most one-third of such decisions turn out right; one-third are minimally effective; and one-third are outright failures.

In no other area of management would we put up with such miserable performance. Indeed, we need not and should not. Managers making people decisions will never be perfect, of course, but they should come pretty close to batting 1,000 – especially since in no other area of management do we know as much.

Some executives' people decisions have, however, approached perfection. At the time of Pearl Harbor, every single general officer in the U.S. Army was overage. Although none of the younger men had been tested in combat or in a significant troup command, the United States came out of World War II with the largest corps of competent general officers any army has ever had. George C. Marshall, the army's chief of staff, had personally chosen each man. Not all were great successes, but practically none were outright failures.

In the 40 or so years during which he ran General Motors, Alfred P. Sloan, Jr. picked every GM executive – down to the manufacturing managers, controllers, engineering managers, and master mechanics at even the smallest accessory division. By today's standards, Sloan's vision and values may seem narrow. They were. He was concerned only with performance in and for GM. Nonetheless, his long-term performance in placing people in the right jobs was flawless.

The basic principles

There is no such thing as an infallible judge of people, at least not on this side of the Pearly Gates. There are, however, a few executives who take their people decisions seriously and work at them.

Marshall and Sloan were about as different as two human beings can be, but they followed, and quite consciously, much the same principles in making people decisions:

☐ If I put a person into a job and he or she does not perform, I have made a mistake. I have no business blaming that person, no business invoking the "Peter Principle," no business complaining. I have made a mistake.

☐ "The soldier has a right to competent command" was already an old maxim at the time of Julius Caesar. It is the duty of managers to make sure that the responsible people in their organizations perform.

☐ Of all the decisions an executive makes, none are as important as the decisions about people because they determine the performance capacity of the organization. Therefore, I'd better make these decisions well.

☐ The one "don't": do not give new people new major assignments, for doing so only compounds the risks. Give this sort of assignment to someone whose behavior and habits you know and who has earned trust and credibility within your organization. Put a high-level newcomer first into an established position where the expectations are known and help is available.

Some of the worst staffing failures I have seen involved brilliant Europeans hired by U.S. companies—one based in Pittsburgh; the other, Chicago—to head up new European ventures. Dr. Hans Schmidt and M. Jean Perrin (only the names are fictitious) were hailed as geniuses when they came in. A year later they were both out, totally defeated.

No one in Pittsburgh had understood that Schmidt's training and temperament would make him sit on a new assignment for the first six or nine months, thinking, studying, planning, getting ready for decisive action. Schmidt, in turn, had never even imagined that Pittsburgh expected instant action and immediate results. No one in Chicago had known that Perrin, while a solid and doggedly purposeful man, was excitable and mercurial, flailing his arms, making speeches about trivia, and sending up one trial balloon after another. Although both men subsequently became highly successful CEOs of major European corporations, both executives were failures in companies that did not know and understand them.

Two other U.S. companies successfully established businesses for the first time in Europe during the same period (the late 1960s and early 1970s). To initiate their projects, each sent to Europe a U.S. executive who had never before worked or lived there but whom people in the head offices knew thoroughly and understood well. In turn the two managers were thoroughly familiar with their companies. At the same time, each organization hired half a dozen young Europeans and placed them in upper-middle executive jobs in the United States. Within a few years, both companies had a solid European business and a trained, seasoned, and trusted corps of executives to run it.

As Winston Churchill's ancestor, the great Duke of Marlborough, observed some three centuries ago, "The basic trouble in coalition warfare is that one has to entrust victory if not one's life, to a fellow commander whom one knows by reputation rather than by performance."

In the corporation as in the military, without personal knowledge built up over a period of time there can be neither trust nor effective communication.

The decision steps

Just as there are only a few basic principles, there are only a few important steps to follow in making effective promotion and staffing decisions:

1 **Think through the assignment.** Job descriptions may last a long time. In one large manufacturing company, for example, the job description for the position of division general manager has hardly changed since the company began to decentralize 30 years ago. Indeed, the job description for bishops in the Roman Catholic church has not changed at all since canon law was first codified in the thirteenth century. But assignments change all the time, and unpredictably.

Once in the early 1940s, I told Alfred Sloan that he seemed to spend an inordinate amount of time pondering the assignment of a fairly low-level job—general sales manager of a small accessory division—before choosing among three equally qualified candidates. "Look at the assignment the last few times we had to fill the same job," Sloan answered. To my surprise, I found that the terms of the assignment were quite different on each occasion.

When putting a man in as division commander during World War II, George Marshall always looked first at the nature of the assignment for the next eighteen months or two years. To raise a division and train it is one assignment. To lead it in combat is quite another. To take command of a division that has been badly mauled and restore its morale and fighting strength is another still.

When the task is to select a new regional sales manager, the responsible executive must first know what the heart of the assignment is: to recruit and train new salespeople because, say, the present sales force is nearing retirement age? Or is it to open up new markets because the company's products, though doing well with old-line industries in the region, have not been able to penetrate new and growing markets? Or, since the bulk of sales still comes from products that are 25 years old, is it to establish a market presence for the company's new products? Each of these is a different assignment and requires a different kind of person.

2 **Look at a number of potentially qualified people.** The controlling word here is "number." Formal qualifications are a minimum for consideration; their absence disqualifies the candidate automatically. Equally important, the person and the assignment need to fit each other. To make an effective decision, an executive should look at three to five qualified candidates.

3 **Think hard about how to look at these candidates.** If an executive has studied the assignment, he or she understands what a new person would need to do with high priority and concentrated effort. The central question is not "What can this or that candidate do or not do?" It is, rather, "What are the strengths each possesses and are these the right strengths for the assignment?" Weaknesses are limitations, which may, of course, rule a candidate out. For instance, a person may be excellently qualified for the technical aspects of a job; but if the assignment requires above all the ability to build a team and this ability is lacking, then the fit is not right.

But effective executives do not start out by looking at weaknesses. You cannot build performance on weaknesses. You can build only on strengths. Both Marshall and Sloan were highly demanding men, but both knew that what matters is the ability to do the assignment. If that exists, the company can always supply the rest. If it does not exist, the rest is useless.

If, for instance, a division needed an officer for a training assignment, Marshall looked for people who could turn recruits into soldiers. Every man that was good at this task usually had serious weaknesses in other areas. One was not particularly effective as a tactical commander and was positively hopeless when it came to strategy. Another had foot-in-mouth disease and got into trouble with the press. A third was vain, arrogant, egotistical, and fought constantly with his commanding officer. Never mind, could he train recruits? If the answer was yes—and especially if the answer was "he's the best"—he got the job.

In picking the members of their cabinets, Franklin Roosevelt and

Harry Truman said, in effect: "Never mind personal weaknesses. Tell me first what each of them can do." It may not be coincidence that these two presidents had the strongest cabinets in twentieth-century U.S. history.

4 **Discuss each of the candidates with several people who have worked with them.** One executive's judgment alone is worthless. Because all of us have first impressions, prejudices, likes, and dislikes, we need to listen to what other people think. When the military picks general officers or the Catholic church picks bishops, this kind of extensive discussion is a formal step in their selection process. Competent executives do it informally. Hermann Abs, the former head of Deutsche Bank, picked more successful chief executives in recent times than anyone else. He personally chose most of the top-level managers who pulled off the postwar German "economic miracle," and he checked out each of them first with three or four of the person's former bosses or colleagues.

5 **Make sure the appointee understands the job.** After the appointee has been in a new job for three or four months, he or she should be focusing on the demands of that job rather than on the requirements of preceeding assignments. It is the executive's responsibility to call that person in and say, "You have now been regional sales manager—or whatever—for three months. What do you have to do to be a success in your new job? Think it through and come back in a week or ten days and show me in writing. But I can tell you one thing right away: the things you did to get the promotion are almost certainly the wrong things to do now."

If you do not follow this step, don't blame the candidate for poor performance. Blame yourself. You have failed in your duty as a manager.

The largest single source of failed promotions—and I know of no greater waste in U.S. management—is the failure to think through, and help others think through, what a new job requires. All too typical is the brilliant former student of mine who telephoned me a few months ago, almost in tears. "I got my first big chance a year ago," he said. "My company made me engineering manager. Now they tell me that I'm through. And yet I've done a better job than ever before. I have actually designed three successful new products for which we'll get patents."

It is only human to say to ourselves, "I must have done something right or I would not have gotten the big new job. Therefore, I had better do more of what I did to get the promotion now that I have it." It is not intuitively obvious to most people that a new and different job requires new and different behavior. Almost 50 years ago, a boss of mine challenged me four months after he had advanced me to a far more responsible position. Until he called me in, I had continued to do what I had done before. To his credit, he understood that it was his responsibility to make me see that a new job means different behavior, a different focus, and different relationships.

The high-risk decisions

Even if executives follow all these steps, some of their people decisions will still fail. These are, for the most part, the high-risk decisions that nevertheless have to be taken.

There is, for example, high risk in picking managers in professional organizations—for a research lab, say, or an engineering or corporate legal department. Professionals do not readily accept as their boss someone whose credentials in the field they do not respect. In choosing a manager of engineering, the choices are therefore limited to the top-flight engineers in the department. Yet there is no correlation (unless it be a negative one) between performance as a bench engineer and performance as a manager. Much the same is true when a high-performing operating manager gets a promotion to a staff job in headquarters or a staff expert moves into a line position. Temperamentally, operating people are frequently unsuited to the tensions, frustrations, and relationships of staff work, and vice versa. The first-rate regional sales manager may well become totally ineffective if promoted into market research, sales forecasting, or pricing.

We do not know how to test or predict whether a person's temperament will suit a new environment. We can find this out only by experience. If a move from one kind of work to another does not pan out, the executive who made the decision has to remove the misfit, and fast. But that executive also has to say, "I made a mistake, and it is my job to correct it." To keep misfits in a job they cannot do is not being kind; it is being cruel. But there is also no reason to let the person go. A company can always use a good bench engineer, a good analyst, a good sales manager. The proper course of action—and it works most times—is to offer the misfit a return to the old job or an equivalent.

People decisions may also fail because a job has become what New England ship captains 150 years ago called a "widow maker." When a clipper ship, no matter how well designed and constructed, began to have fatal "accidents," the owners did not redesign or rebuild the ship. They broke it up as fast as possible.

Widow makers—that is, jobs that regularly defeat even good people—appear most often when a company grows or changes fast. For instance, in the 1960s and early 1970s, the job of "international vice president" in U.S. banks became a widow maker. It had always been an easy job to fill. In fact, it had long been considered a job in which banks could safely put "also rans" and could expect them to perform well. Then, suddenly, the job began to defeat one new incumbent after another. What had happened, as hindsight now tells us, is that international activity quickly and without warning became an integral part of the daily business of major banks and their corporate customers. What had been until then an easy job became, literally, a "nonjob" that nobody could do.

Whenever a job defeats two people in a row, who in their earlier assignments had performed well, a company has a widow maker on its hands. When this happens, a responsible executive should not ask the headhunter for a universal genius. Instead abolish the job. Any job that ordinarily competent people cannot perform is a job that cannot be staffed. Unless changed, it will predictably defeat the third incumbent the way it defeated the first two.

Making the right people decisions is the ultimate means of controlling an organization well. Such decisions reveal how competent management is, what its values are, and whether it takes its job seriously. No matter how hard managers try to keep their decisions a secret—and some still try hard—people decisions cannot be hidden. They are eminently visible.

Executives often cannot judge whether a strategic move is a wise one. Nor are they necessarily interested. "I don't know why we are buying this business in Australia, but it won't interfere with what we are doing here in Fort Worth" is a common reaction. But when the same executives read that "Joe Smith has been made controller in the XYZ division," they usually know Joe much better than top management does. These executives should be able to say, "Joe deserves the promotion; he is an excellent choice—just the person that division needs to get the controls appropriate for its rapid growth."

If, however, Joe got promoted because he is a politician, everybody will know it. They will all say to themselves, "Okay, that is the way to get ahead in this company." They will despise their management for forcing them to become politicians but will either quit or become politicians themselves in the end. As we have known for a long time, people in organizations tend to behave as they see others being rewarded. And when the rewards go to nonperformance, to flattery, or to mere cleverness, the organization will soon decline into nonperformance, flattery, or cleverness.

Executives who do not make the effort to get their people decisions right do more than risk poor performance. They risk losing their organization's respect. ▽

Reprint 85406

Skilled incompetence

Chris Argyris

"Managers who are skilled communicators may also be good at covering up real problems."

The ability to get along with others is always an asset, right? Wrong. By adeptly avoiding conflict with coworkers, some executives eventually wreak organizational havoc. And it's their very adeptness that's the problem. The explanation for this lies in what I call skilled incompetence, whereby managers use practiced routine behavior (skill) to produce what they do not intend (incompetence). We can see this happen when managers talk to each other in ways that are seemingly candid and straightforward. What we don't see so clearly is how managers' skills can become institutionalized and create disastrous side effects in their organizations. Consider this familiar situation:

The entrepreneur-CEO of a fast-growing medium-sized company brought together his bright, dedicated, hardworking top managers to devise a new strategic plan. The company had grown at about 45% per year, but fearing that it was heading into deep administrative trouble, the CEO had started to rethink his strategy. He decided he wanted to restructure his organization along more rational, less ad hoc, lines. As he saw it, the company was split between the sales-oriented people who sell off-the-shelf products and the people producing custom services who are oriented toward professionals. And each group was suspicious of the other. He wanted the whole group to decide what kind of company it was going to run.

His immediate subordinates agreed that they must develop a vision and make some strategic decisions. They held several long meetings to do this. Although the meetings were pleasant enough and no

Chris Argyris is the James Bryant Conant Professor of Education and Organizational Behavior at the Harvard University Graduate School of Education. His studies have focused on how people learn and have resulted in a long list of articles—many of which have appeared in HBR—and books, the latest of which is Strategy, Change, and Defensive Routines *(Ballinger, 1985).*

one seemed to be making life difficult for anyone else, they concluded with no agreements or decisions. "We end up compiling lists of issues but not deciding," said one vice president. Another added, "And it gets pretty discouraging when this happens every time we meet." A third worried aloud, "If you think we are discouraged, how do you think the people below us feel who watch us repeatedly fail?"

This is a group of executives who are at the top, who respect each other, who are highly committed, and who agree that developing a vision and strategy is critical. Yet whenever they meet, they fail to create the vision and the strategy they desire. What is going on here? Are the managers really so incompetent? If so, why?

What causes incompetence

At first, the executives in the previous example believed that they couldn't formulate and implement a good strategic plan because they lacked sound financial data. So they asked the financial vice president to reorganize and reissue the data. Everyone agreed he did a superb job.

But the financial executive reported to me, "Our problem is *not* the absence of financial data. I can flood them with data. We lack a vision of what kind of company we want to be and a strategy. Once we produce those, I can supply the necessary data." The other executives reluctantly agreed.

After several more meetings in which nothing got done, a second explanation emerged. It had to do with the personalities of the individuals and the way they work with each other. The CEO explained, "This is a group of lovable guys with very strong egos. They are competitive, bright, candid, and dedicated. But when we meet, we seem to go in circles; we are not prepared to give in a bit and make the necessary compromises."

Is this explanation valid? Should the top managers become less competitive? I'm not sure. Some management groups are not good at problem solving and decision making precisely because the participants have weak egos and are uncomfortable with competition.

If personality were really the problem, the cure would be psychotherapy. And it's simply not true that to be more effective, executives need years on the couch. Besides, pinpointing personality as the issue hides the real culprit.

The culprit is skill

Let's begin by asking whether counterproductive behavior is also natural and routine. Does everyone seem to be acting sincerely? Do things go wrong even though the managers are not being destructively manipulative and political?

For the executive group, the answer to these questions is yes. Their motives were decent, and they were at their personal best. Their actions were spontaneous, automatic, and unrehearsed. They acted in milliseconds; they were skilled communicators.

How can skillful actions be counterproductive? When we're skillful we usually produce what we intend. So, in a sense, did the executives. In this case, the skilled behavior – the spontaneous and automatic responses – was meant to avoid upset and conflict at the meetings. The unintended by-products are what cause trouble. Because the executives don't say what they really mean or test the assumptions they really hold, their skills inhibit a resolution of the important intellectual issues embedded in developing the strategy. Thus the meetings end with only lists and no decisions.

This pattern of failure is not only typical for this group of managers. It happens to people in all kinds of organizations regardless of age, gender, educational background, wealth, or position in the hierarchy. Let me illustrate with another example that involves the entire organizational culture at the upper levels. Here we'll begin to see how people's tendency to avoid conflict, to duck the tough issues, becomes institutionalized and leads to a culture that can't tolerate straight talk.

Where the skillful thrive

The top management of a large, decentralized corporation was having difficulty finding out what some of its division presidents were up to. Time and time again the CEO would send memos to the presidents asking for information, and time and time again they'd send next to nothing in return. But other people at headquarters accepted this situation as normal. When asked why they got so little direct communication from their division heads, they'd respond, "That's the way we do things around here."

Here is an organization that isn't talking to itself. The patterns that managers set up among themselves have become institutionalized, and what were once characteristic personal exchanges have now become organizational defensive routines. Before I go on to describe what these routines look like, let's look at how this situation arose.

Built into decentralization is the age-old tug between autonomy and control: superiors want no surprises, subordinates want to be left alone. The subordinates push for autonomy; they assert that by leaving them alone, top management will show its trust from a distance. The superiors, on the other hand, try to keep control through information systems. The subordinates see the control devices as confirming their suspicions – their superiors don't trust them.

Many executives I have observed handle this tension by pretending that the tension is not there. They act as if everyone were in accord and trust that no one will point out disagreements and thereby rock the boat. At the same time, however, they do feel the tension and can't help but soft-pedal their talk. They send mixed messages. (See the insert on chaos.)

The CEO in this example kept saying to his division presidents, "I mean it – you run the show down there." The division presidents, wanting to prove their mettle, believed him until an important issue came up. When it did the CEO, concerned about the situation and forgetting that he wanted his division chiefs to be innovative, would make phone calls and send memos seeking information.

Defensive routines emerge

One of the most powerful ways people deal with potential embarrassment is to create "organizational defensive routines." I define these as any action or policy designed to avoid surprise, embarrassment, or threat. But they also prevent learning and

Four easy steps to chaos

How does a manager send mixed messages? It takes skill. Here are four rules:

1

Design a clearly ambiguous message. For example, "Be innovative and take risks, but be careful" is a message that says in effect, "Go, but go just so far" without specifying how far far is. The ambiguity and imprecision cover the speaker who can't know ahead of time what is too far.

The receiver, on the other hand, clearly understands the ambiguity and imprecision. Moreover, he or she knows that a request for more precision would likely be interpreted as a sign of immaturity or inexperience. And the receivers may also need an out some day and may want to keep the message imprecise and ambiguous. Receivers don't want "far" defined any more clearly than the senders do.

2

Ignore any inconsistencies in the message. When people send mixed messages, they usually do it spontaneously and with no sign that the message is mixed. Indeed, if they did appear to hesitate, they would defeat their purpose of maintaining control. Even worse, they might appear weak.

3

Make the ambiguity and inconsistency in the message undiscussable. The whole point of sending a mixed message is to avoid dealing with a situation straight on. The sender does not want the message's mixedness exposed. An executive is not about to send a mixed message and then ask, "Do you find my message inconsistent and ambiguous?" The executive also renders the message undiscussable by the very natural way of sending it. To challenge the innocence of the sender is to imply that the sender is duplicitous—not a likely thing for a subordinate to do.

4

Make the undiscussability also undiscussable. One of the best ways to do this is to send the mixed message in a setting that is not conducive to open inquiry, such as a large meeting or a group where people of unequal organizational status are present. No one wants to launder linen in public. While they are sending mixed messages during a meeting, people rarely reflect on their actions or talk about how the organizational culture, including the meeting, makes discussing the undiscussable difficult.

division heads who are directed by mixed messages. They feel a lack of trust and are suspicious of their boss's intentions but they must, nonetheless, find ways to live with the mixed messages. So they "explain" the messages to themselves and to their subordinates. These explanations often sound like this:

> "Corporate never *really* meant decentralization."

> "Corporate is willing to trust divisions when the going is smooth, but not when it's rough."

> "Corporate is more concerned about the stock market than about us."

Of course, the managers rarely test their hypotheses about corporate motives with top executives. If discussing mixed messages among themselves would be uncomfortable, then public testing of the validity of these explanations would be embarrassing.

But now the division heads are in a double bind. On the one hand, if they go along unquestioningly, they may lose their autonomy and their subordinates will see them as having little influence with corporate. On the other, if the division executives do not comply with orders from above, headquarters will think they are recalcitrant, and if noncompliance continues, disloyal.

Top management is in a similar predicament. It senses that division managers have suspicions about headquarters' motives and are covering them up. If headquarters makes its impression known, though, the division heads may get upset. If the top does not say anything, the division presidents could infer full agreement when there is none. Usually, in the name of keeping up good relations, the top covers up its predicament.

Soon, people in the divisions learn to live with their binds by generating further explanations. For example, they may eventually conclude that openness is a strategy that top management has devised intentionally to cover up its unwillingness to be influenced.

Since this conclusion is based on the assumption that people at the top are covering up, managers won't test it either. Since neither headquarters nor division executives discuss or resolve the attributions or the frustrations, both may eventually stop communicating regularly and openly. Once in place, the climate of mistrust makes it more likely that the issues become undiscussable.

Now both headquarters and division managers have attitudes, assumptions, and actions that create self-fulfilling and self-sealing processes that each sees the other as creating.

thereby prevent organizations from investigating or eliminating the underlying problems.

Defensive routines are systemic in that most people within the company adhere to them. People leave the organization and new ones arrive, yet the defensive routines remain intact.

To see the impact of the defensive routines and the range of their effects, let's return to the

"It's an interesting invention, but because of some irregularities, the elders have decided to have it recalled."

Under these conditions, it is not surprising to find that superiors and subordinates hold both good and bad feelings about each other. For example, they may say about each other: "They are bright and well intentioned but they have a narrow, parochial view"; or "They are interested in the company's financial health but they do not understand how they are harming earnings in the long run"; or "They are interested in people but they pay too little attention to the company's development."

My experience is that people cannot build on their appreciation of others without first overcoming their suspicions. But to overcome what they don't like, people must be able to discuss it. And this requirement violates the undiscussability rule embedded in the organizational defensive routines.

Is there any organization that does not have these hang-ups and problems? Some people suggest that getting back to basics will open lines of communication. But the proffered panacea does not go far enough; it does not deal with the underlying patterns. Problems won't be solved by simply correcting one isolated instance of poor performance.

When CEOs I have observed declared war against organizational barriers to candor and demanded that people get back to basics, most often they implemented the new ideas with the old skills. People changed whatever they could and learned to cover their asses even more skillfully. The freedom to ques-

tion and to confront is crucial, but it is inadequate. To overcome skilled incompetence, people have to learn new skills—to ask the questions behind the questions.

Defensive routines exist. They are undiscussable. They proliferate and grow underground. And the social pollution is hard to identify until something occurs that blows things open. Often that something is a glaring error whose results cannot be hidden. The recent space shuttle disaster is an example. Only after the accident occurred were the mixed messages and defensive routines used during the decision to launch exposed. The disaster made it legitimate for outsiders to require insiders to discuss the undiscussable. (By the way, writing a tighter set of controls and requiring better communication won't solve the problem. Tighter controls will only enlarge the book of rules that William Rogers, chairman of the president's committee to investigate the Challenger disaster, acknowledged can be a cure worse than the illness. He pointed out that in his Navy years, when the players went by the book, things only got worse.)

Managers do not have the choice to ignore the organizational problems that these self-sealing loops create. They may be able to get away with it today, but they're creating a legacy for those who will come after them.

How to become unskilled

The top management group I described at the beginning of this article decided to learn new skills by examining the defenses they created in their own meetings.

First, they arranged a two-day session away from the office for which they wrote a short case beforehand. The purpose of these cases was twofold. First, they allowed the executives to develop a collage of the problems they thought were critical. Not surprisingly, in this particular group at least half wrote on issues related to the product versus custom service conflict. Second, the cases provided a kind of window into the prevailing rules and routines the executives used. The form of the case was as follows:

1   In one paragraph describe a key organizational problem as you see it.

2   In attacking the problem, assume you could talk to whomever you wish. Describe, in a paragraph or so, the strategy you would use in this meeting.

3   Next, split your page into two columns. On the right-hand side, write how you would begin the meeting: what you would actually say. Then write

what you believe the other(s) would say. Then write your response to their response. Continue writing this scenario for two or so double-spaced typewritten pages.

4   In the left-hand column write any of your ideas or feelings that you would not communicate for whatever reason.

The executives reported that they became engrossed in writing the cases. Some said that the very writing of their case was an eye-opener. Moreover, once the stories were distributed, the reactions were jocular. They enjoyed them: "Great, Joe does this all the time"; "Oh, there's a familiar one"; "All salespeople and no listeners"; "Oh my God, this is us."

What is the advantage of using the cases? Crafted and written by the executives themselves, they become vivid examples of skilled incompctcncc. They illustrate the skill with which each executive sought to avoid upsetting the other while trying to change the other's mind. The cases also illustrate their incompetence. By their own analysis, what they did upset the others, created suspicion, and made it less likely that their views would prevail.

The cases are also very important learning devices. During a meeting, it is difficult to slow down behavior produced in milliseconds, to reflect on it, and to change it. For one thing, it's hard to pay attention to interpersonal actions and to substantive issues at the same time.

A collage from several cases appears in the *Exhibit*. It was written by executives who believed the company should place a greater emphasis on custom service.

The cases written by individuals who supported the product strategy did not differ much. They too were trying to persuade, sell, or cajole their fellow officers. Their left-hand columns were similar.

In analyzing their left-hand columns, the executives found that each side blamed the other for the difficulties, and they used the same reasons. For example, each side said:

"If you insist on your position, you'll harm the morale I've built."

"Don't hand me that line. You know what I'm talking about."

"Why don't you take off your blinders and wear a company hat?"

"It upsets me when I think of how they think."

"I'm really trying hard, but I'm beginning to feel this is hopeless."

Exhibit	Case of the custom-service advocate

Thoughts and feelings	Actual conversation
He's not gcing to like this topic, but we have to discuss it. I doubt that he will take a company perspective, but I should be positive.	**I:** Hi Bill. I appreciate having the opportunity to talk with you about this custom service versus product problem. I'm sure that both of us want to resolve it in the best interests of the company.
	Bill: I'm always glad to talk about it, as you well know.
I better go slow. Let me ease in.	**I:** There are a rising number of situations where our clients are asking for custom service and rejecting the off-the-shelf products. I worry that your salespeople will play an increasingly peripheral role in the future.
	Bill: I don't understand. Tell me more.
Like hell you don't understand. I wish there was a way I could be more gentle.	**I:** Bill, I'm sure you are aware of the changes [I explain].
	Bill: No, I don't see it that way. My salespeople are the key to the future.
There he goes, thinking like a salesman and not like a corporate officer.	**I:** Well, let's explore that a bit.

These cases effectively illustrate the influence of skilled incompetence. In crafting the cases, the executives were trying not to upset the others and at the same time were trying to change their minds. This process requires skill. Yet the skill they used in the cases has the unintended side effects I talked about. In the cases, the others became upset and dug in their heels without changing their minds.

Here's a real problem. These executives and all the others I've studied to date can't prevent the counterproductive consequences until and unless they learn new skills. Nor will it work to bypass the skilled incompetence by focusing on the business problems, such as, in this case, developing a business strategy.

The answer is unlearning

The crucial step is for executives to begin to revise how they'd tackle their case. At their two-day seminar each manager selected an episode he wished to redesign so that it would not have the unhappy result it currently produced.

In rewriting their cases, the managers realized that they would have to slow things down. They could not produce a new conversation in the milliseconds in which they were accustomed to speak. This troubled them a bit because they were impatient to learn. They had to keep reminding themselves that learning new skills meant they had to slow down.

Each manager took a different manager's case and crafted a new conversation to help the writer of the episode. After five minutes or so, they showed their designs to the writer. In the process of discussing these new versions, the writer learned a lot about how to redesign his words. And, as they discovered the bugs in their suggestions and the way they made them, the designers also learned a lot.

The dialogues were constructive, cooperative, and helpful. Typical comments were:

> "If you want to reach me, try it the way Joe just said."

> "I realize your intentions are good, but those words push my button."

> "I understand what you're trying to say, but it doesn't work for me. How about trying it this way?"

> "I'm surprised at how much my new phrases contain the old messages. This will take time."

Practice is important. Most people require as much practice to overcome skilled incompetence as to play a not-so-decent game of tennis. But it doesn't need to happen all at once. Once managers are committed to change, the practice can occur in actual business meetings where executives set aside some time to reflect on their actions and to correct them.

But how does unlearning skilled incompetence lead to fewer organizational snafus? The first step is to make sure executives are aware of defensive routines that surround the organizational problems that they are trying to solve. One way to do this is to observe them in the making. For example, during a meeting of the top line and corporate staff officers in our large decentralized organization, the CEO asked why the line and staff were having problems working effectively. They identified at least four causes:

> The organization's management philosophy and policies are inadequate.

> Corporate staff roles overlap and lead to confusion.

> Staff lacks clear-cut authority when dealing with line.

> Staff has inadequate contact with top line officers.

The CEO appointed two task forces to come up with solutions. Several months later, the entire group met for a day and hammered out a solution that was acceptable to all.

This story has two features that I would highlight. First, the staff-line problems are typical. Second, the story has a happy ending. The organization got to the root of its problems.

But there is a question that must be answered in order to get at the organizational defensive routines. Why did all the managers—both upper and lower—adhere to, implement, and maintain inadequate policies and confusing roles in the first place?

Why open this can of worms if we have already solved the problem? Because defensive routines prevent executives from making honest decisions. Managers who are skilled communicators may also be good at covering up real problems. If we don't work hard at reducing defensive routines, they will thrive—ready to undermine this solution and cover up other conflicts. ▽

Reprint 86501

There is great skill in knowing how to conceal one's skill.

La Rochefoucauld

READ THE FINE PRINT

REPRINTS
Telephone: 617-495-6192
Fax: 617-495-6985

Current and past articles
are available, as is an
annually updated index.
Discounts apply to
large-quantity purchases.

Please send orders to
HBR Reprints
Harvard Business School
Publishing Division
Boston, MA 02163.

HOW CAN *HARVARD BUSINESS REVIEW* ARTICLES WORK FOR YOU?

For years, we've printed a microscopically small notice on the editorial credits page of the *Harvard Business Review* alerting our readers to the availability of *HBR* articles.

Now we invite you to take a closer look at some of the many ways you can put this hard-working business tool to work for you.

IN THE CORPORATE CLASSROOM.

There's no more effective, or cost-effective, way to supplement your corporate training programs than in-depth, incisive *HBR* articles.

Affordable and accessible, it's no wonder hundreds of companies and consulting organizations use *HBR* articles as a centerpiece for management training.

IN-BOX INNOVATION.

Where do your company's movers and shakers get their big ideas? Many find the inspiration for innovation in the pages of *HBR*. They then share the wealth and spread the word by distributing *HBR* articles to company colleagues.

IN MARKETING AND SALES SUPPORT.

HBR articles are a substantive leave-behind to your sales calls. And they can add credibility to your direct mail campaigns. They demonstrate that your company is on the leading edge of business thinking.

CREATE CUSTOM ARTICLES.

If you want to pack even greater power in your punch, personalize *HBR* articles with your company's name or logo. And get the added benefit of putting your organization's name before your customers.

AND THERE ARE 500 MORE REASONS IN THE *HBR CATALOG*.

In all, the *Harvard Business Review Catalog* lists articles on over 500 different subjects. Plus, you'll find books and videos on subjects you need to know.

The catalog is yours for just $8.00. To order *HBR* articles or the *HBR Catalog* (No. 21019), call 617-495-6192. Please mention telephone order code 025A when placing your order. Or FAX us at 617-495-6985.

And start putting *HBR* articles to work for you.

**Harvard Business School
Publications**

Call 617-495-6192 to order the *HBR Catalog*.

(Prices and terms subject to change.)

YOU SAID: AND WE SAID:

"Give us training tools that are relevant to our business...ones we can use *now*."

"We need new cases that stimulate meaningful discussion."

"It can't be a catalog of canned programs... everything we do is custom."

"Make it a single source for up-to-date materials ...on the most current business topics."

"Better yet if it's from a reputable business school. That adds credibility."

"Introducing the Harvard Business School Publications Corporate Training and Development Catalog."

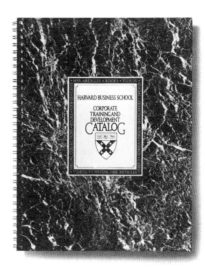

You asked for it. And now it's here.

The Harvard Business School Publications Corporate Training and Development Catalog is created exclusively for those who design and develop custom training programs.

It's filled cover-to-cover with valuable materials you can put to work on the spot. You'll find a comprehensive selection of cases, *Harvard Business Review* articles, videos, books, and more.

Our new catalog covers the critical management topics affecting corporations today, like Leadership, Quality, Global Business, Marketing, and Strategy, to name a few. And it's all organized, indexed, and cross-referenced to make it easy for you to find precisely what you need.

HOW TO ORDER.

To order by FAX, dial 617-495-6985. Or call 617-495-6192. Please mention telephone order code 132A. Or send this coupon with your credit card information to: HBS Publications Corporate Training and Development Catalog, Harvard Business School Publishing Division, Operations Department, Boston, MA 02163. **All orders must be prepaid.**

Order No.	Title	Qty. ×	Price +	Shipping* =	Total
39001	Catalog		$8		

Prices and terms subject to change.
*For orders outside Continental U.S.: 20% for surface delivery. Allow 3-6 months. *Express Deliveries* billed at cost; all foreign orders not designating express delivery will be sent by surface mail.

☐ VISA ☐ American Express ☐ MasterCard

Card Number_____ Exp. Date_____

Signature_____

Telephone_____ FAX_____

Name_____

Organization_____

Street_____

City_____ State/Zip_____

Country_____ ☐ Home Address ☐ Organization Address

Please Reference Telephone Order Code 132A

Harvard Business School Publications